C000090467

IN YOUR FACE

IN YOUR
FACE
A RUGBY ODYSSEY

RICHARD COCKERILL with **MICHAEL TANNER**

MAINSTREAM
PUBLISHING

EDINBURGH AND LONDON

Copyright © Richard Cockerill and Michael Tanner, 1999
All rights reserved
The moral right of the author has been asserted

First published in Great Britain in 1999 by
MAINSTREAM PUBLISHING COMPANY
(EDINBURGH) LTD
7 Albany Street
Edinburgh EH1 3UG

ISBN 1 84018 266 0

No part of this book may be reproduced or transmitted in
any form or by any means without written permission from
the publisher, except by a reviewer who wishes to quote brief
passages in connection with a review written for insertion in
a magazine, newspaper or broadcast

A catalogue record for this book is available
from the British Library

Typeset in Bembo
Printed and bound in Great Britain by Butler & Tanner Ltd

Dedicated to my parents,
for their total support − in all circumstances!

CONTENTS

ONE

WEARING THE RED ROSE

W HEN I was told I'd made the England squad for the 1999 World Cup, the news came not from England coach Clive Woodward but from my Leicester and England team-mate Graham Rowntree.

The squad was meant to have been announced on 29 August, a Sunday night, at 9 p.m. I switched on my computer to look at the e-mails, and one said the squad was not now going to be announced until 5 p.m. the following day. I wasn't that anxious about whether I'd be included – but you never know. I had not been involved at all in the warm-up international against the USA and had not started the second warm-up game versus Canada. And the weekend of the USA match I'd received an 'interesting' e-mail from Clive which said something like: 'If you insist on continuing to play the style of rugby with England that you play with Leicester, I cannot pick you.' A lot of it is mind games – Clive trying to wind his players up – but people do tend to be a little braver when writing to you instead of telling you face to face. Some of the press were also suggesting I wasn't the man for the job of first-choice hooker. They were busy talking up Phil Greening, an old rival of mine. Yet I'd accumulated 23 caps: I'd been there and done the job. Quite simply, it was payback time. With my personality and rugby CV, the press are always dying for something or other to go wrong so they can heap abuse on me. I'm an easy target. I'd never claimed I was the undisputed first-choice hooker. The press stick those labels on you – and then they turn them around to use against you, even though it's something you never said. If a better player is picked ahead of me, I'll hold my hands up. But I badly wanted to play in this World Cup. I'm 28 years old and I don't think I'm going to get another opportunity. Phil Greening will get another crack – when the next one comes around he'll be the same age as I am now. This World Cup was a once-in-a-lifetime thing as far as I was concerned and I wanted to be a part of it so much.

Anyway, I thought, what's another day? We were due back at Lympstone, the Royal Marines training centre in Devon, on the Tuesday – that is, if you were in the final squad – so on the Monday I was at my 'student' house, near Leicester City's football ground, doing a spot of DIY, a bit of painting and decorating and what-have-you. Then Graham rings me to fix up a lift for Tuesday – and that's how I knew I was in. Everything seems to be done by computer these days but they can leave you in limbo. Tim Stimpson's wasn't working, so he rang Will Greenwood to find out the composition of the squad, thinking he'd done enough to be included. Will had the unenviable task of telling him he'd been dropped, which wasn't an ideal situation for either of them to be put in.

Probably from the age of 15 or 16 I began to think I'd a realistic chance of one day playing for England. I got through the town trials, Warwickshire and the Midlands, to win my cap at U16 level. I got the taste for it. You get the blazer, the shirt and all your kit, and you're so proud to wear it. You think, 'I like this, I want more of it!' I didn't get picked at Colts level, mainly, I tend to think, because I was abusive to some people in positions of power. But I did win selection for the U21 and Emerging England sides later on, and then, in 1995, I played for the A side against Italy. The A team is a very difficult set-up. You're so close and yet so far away; you are a second-class citizen in the A side because you don't get the same kit or treatment or hotels, and you have relatively little preparation time together – and yet you're expected to perform, often in quite difficult environments. In many respects, playing for the A team is more difficult than playing for the full side. I must have sat on the bench 20 or more times but I was picked to start in only six games. No one ever told me why. I just wasn't picked. There was always some new kid who would come through and leapfrog me – Kevin Dunn, Mark Regan, Phil Greening or who-ever. There was always somebody else. It seemed they were afraid to leave me out completely but they would never summon up the nerve to put me on from the start.

It was all very frustrating, but I'd decided at a very early age that I'd never change the way I played or behaved just to suit others. Some of the selectors thought I was too much of a Jack-the-lad, someone who talked too much and was potentially a liability on the pitch because of my aggressive attitude and habit of conceding penalties. But in the old days some of the RFU people were so pompous and old-fashioned it just wasn't true. For example, two guys came out to Italy with the 'A' team. One of them was so fat he had to have two seats on the plane! People like me and Daz Garforth, who were self-employed, were losing money to play, so we asked these blokes whether we shouldn't at least be paid for loss of earnings. This fat one says: 'No, pulling on the shirt should be enough.' It's total bullshit to say the reward of wearing the shirt is enough. It seemed as though it was all right for the blokes who could afford to play for England to represent their country but those who needed to work couldn't afford to play for England. I looked at this guy and told him: 'You fat f***er, you should f*** off back to your ivory tower and stay there!'

Some of these committee men aren't much better today. When I scored a try against Ireland at Twickenham in 1988, I kicked the ball into the stands in jubilation. After the match, this committee man comes up to me and says: 'You shouldn't have done that. If that ball had struck someone drinking a cup of hot coffee the RFU would have been liable for compensation had the person been scalded.' I ask you! I just walked away.

This sort of attitude didn't do my prospects any good. There was a tour to Australia and Fiji in the summer of 1995 and although I'd shared the season's matches with Regan, they dropped me for the tour in favour of Gareth Adams, a converted flanker, from Bath. Peter Rossborough, the former England full-back, was the man in charge. He was a Coventry man, which I thought might work to my advantage as I'd once played for the club, but it turned out he was no fan of mine at all. He rang to tell me I was a liability, too abrasive, too feisty and I had spoken disrespectfully to committee men. John Elliott, another selector, didn't rate me either – and he was a former Leicester hooker! He thought I was too small and didn't have the right attitude. I felt a bit aggrieved that I'd been denied my chance. What pisses me off about selectors at times is that they never gave me the chance to prove myself one way or the other. It was the Neil Back syndrome: if you didn't fit into the category they wanted, they discarded you without really seeing what you could do. If it was up to Peter Rossborough and John Elliott I'd have never won a full cap. Since I've won international honours I've given John Elliott a piece of my mind and told him where he stands in my estimation. I told him he wrote players off too quickly just because they didn't say please and thank you or wear their collar and tie at the correct time. I said all of that is bullshit. If someone has talent, the selectors and coaches should harness that talent – and discipline them afterwards. If I was too opinionated or too aggressive – which I don't think you ever can be – those qualities should have been channelled in the right direction rather than stifled.

Of course, Regan had a decent tour and was capped the following season, eventually making the Lions tour to South Africa in 1997. That really pissed me off, but with Regan out of the reckoning, Phil Greening and I were the only options to go on the short tour of Argentina that same summer. This was my big chance – as I saw it – to get capped. Greening went as first choice and I sat on the bench for the first game. We struggled in the scrum a little and I played in the next two matches, doing pretty well, I reckoned. I thought I'd played well enough to get the nod for the first Test in Buenos Aires. I was gutted when Jack Rowell, still the coach at that time, told me I was not in the team. He just said, 'We'll do our best to get you on for a cap as a consolation.' Daz was playing but I was really annoyed. In circumstances like these, you're almost willing the player in your position to be injured – without getting them killed, of course! You're constantly watching them at every breakdown to see if they're suffering. After about 20 minutes Greening got concussed. He made a lazy tackle and got knocked backwards. His legs were like rubber. A few minutes later, they came over for a lineout and he couldn't remember the calls – so I went on. I could have cried at that moment, thinking of what I'd gone through to get to this. I was elated for myself, my mum and dad, all the boys at Newbold – my home village and first club – and everyone who had helped me get there. My lifetime's ambition was achieved. The buzz I got was beyond experience. My immediate thought was that I was an England player now and there was a job to be done. It was a case of getting on with it rather than dwelling on my achievement. I had 60 minutes of the game to play against a very tough and physical Argentinian side. I was mad for it! There was nothing I wouldn't have done. I'd have given my life that day. I got my hands on the ball a few times and, I think, did pretty well – and we won 46–22.

Six or seven of us were capped that afternoon – including Martin Corry, subsequently a Leicester team-mate – and we were all presented with our caps and ties in the dressing-room, which is far better than receiving them at the official dinner in the evening, because this way you're just sharing the moment with the boys you've done it with out on the pitch. You wear your cap all night and have to sing a song to celebrate the occasion. Some people have found this more nerve-wracking than playing the match. I know Neil Back did, for example. I sang 'American Pie'. Daz told me I'd not to pay for a single drink all night because he was buying. Along with the other prop, Kevin Yates, of Bath, who was also a new cap, we went to a nightclub and I got completely bladdered. The tradition is that if someone buys you a drink you have what they're drinking, so I was consuming everything and anything.

We travelled the next day for a midweek game and on arrival there was a team-run for the midweek side. Of course, Phil

Greening wasn't allowed to train, was he, so after being out on the piss till five in the morning I had to do the team-run. There's the Test side down one end of the pitch playing 'touch' and I'm down the other end working my bollocks off and feeling so ill it's not true. I was spewing on the touchline before throwing in! We lost Ollie Redman and Mike Catt to the Lions before the second Test, which was a blow to our chances, and the Argentinians were really up for the game because they'd been slated in the press for their display in the first Test. The atmosphere was really intimidating to say the least. The crowd was fanatical and hurling limes at me as I was throwing in – the English could hardly expect to be popular out there, could they? We ended up losing 13–33.

I came back from Argentina with two caps, a very proud Englishman. I wanted more but, realistically, my chances of playing for England again appeared slim. Even though I was down the pecking order, I was not about to throw in the towel. I'd never walked away from a scrap and wasn't about to start at the age of 26.

TWO

THE URGE TO COMPETE

RUGBY just seemed to fit my personality. I enjoyed the competitiveness of it. If there was a fight at school or on the village green, I was always in the middle of it. So rugby appealed to me straightaway, this kind of – what's the best way to put it? – this sort of controlled violence. I had a very short temper. I do lose it quickly, though I'd say in my defence that I do regain my composure just as quickly – which is what people see on the rugby field today where I'm concerned. Anyway, in rugby it seemed you were allowed to do whatever you wanted, basically, and you could get away with it, which you weren't allowed to do in the playground or in society generally. That appealed to me. I took to it like a duck to water, I don't know why. I revelled in all the physical stuff, enjoyed the weight training, enjoyed the scrummaging and enjoyed intimidating other people.

I'm not sure where I got my competitive edge from. It may have had something to do with my brother John. He was tall, dark and handsome, and went to school at Lawrence Sherriff in Rugby, where he played as a centre. I was the short dumpy one who was not good at anything and went to Harris Church of England, a comprehensive school in Rugby. John is two years older than me and I think having an older brother develops a certain competitiveness. You're always competing with him to get attention from your parents, or thinking 'I can do that', because older brothers tend to do things first and you want to copy them. We get on now, but as kids and teenagers we were always fighting with each other. I didn't really like my brother, to be honest, as a kid and as a teenager. He never picked on me, he's not that sort of person. It was situations like when my mum and dad went out and left me in the house at the age of 13 or 14 and I'd want to watch something on television, he'd want to watch something else and we'd end up in a big punch-up. And he's not a violent person. We're totally chalk and cheese in that respect. He'll avoid violence at any cost whereas it never really bothers me. But I had to compete with him. For his fourteenth birthday, for example, John got some weight-training equipment, so I wanted to do it as well. Straightaway I got some weight-training kit for my thirteenth birthday.

We lived in a tiny hamlet called Leamington Hastings, midway between Leamington and Rugby, where my parents still live to this day. To begin with, I'd no interest in rugby. My team game was football. I played for Wolston Dynamos, a few miles down the road, with my best mate, Richard Cook, who was the best man at my wedding. I played anywhere they'd have me − in goal, in defence, up front. I'm not particularly a naturally talented sportsman. I've got quite good eye-to-ball co-ordination but that's about it. I'd been to only two rugby games in my life: Coventry against Bristol in the semi-final of the John Player Cup and Midlands versus Australia, which was the game in which Peter Wheeler got sent off. Anyway, when I got to Harris C of E it was a choice between rugby or cross-country, and I hated running around so it had to be rugby. The headmaster was a man called Brian Poxon, who was rugby through and through. He encouraged us a lot, as did Phil Hall, another teacher there who'd played for Rugby Lions as a prop. He was a great guy and devoted a lot of his own time to helping us. He's finished with the job now because of the way teaching has gone. I wouldn't go so far as to say he was my mentor or an inspiration to me, because I don't think I've ever had one, to be truthful.

I seemed to spend most of my time in Brian Poxon's office getting a bollocking. I hate education. I hated school. I hate writing and I hate reading. It just doesn't appeal to me whatsoever. I got no GCSEs. I wasn't a drop-out – I took the exams – but I didn't even pass woodwork because I didn't want to do the written stuff. All I wanted to do at school was leave and go to work! Looking back, in some ways I wish I was academically inclined because it is fantastic to have an education. At the time, though, never having met a student, I hated students. Now I'm married to a former student and, seeing the life they lead at closer quarters, I think it's a great opportunity and a marvellous life. I've met a lot of academics but their life skills are often nil. My life skills and social skills are very good, which has probably helped me a lot. Some people watch me play rugby and think I must be dull and a hooligan. I'm not intellectual and I'm not bright academically, but in life skills, getting on with people, doing business with people, doing deals and making money, I'm very sharp. Education is not the be all and end all. There is a life beyond education. People should never try to be things they're not. That's how I try to lead my life.

Many of my teachers were just bullies as far as I'm concerned. One maths teacher, Mr Burgess, was a right little dictator. I'd done something wrong one day and I had to go and stand outside the staff room all lunchtime. When the bell rang for afternoon classes I left for my next lesson. Pretty soon a kid came into my class and said Mr Burgess wanted to see me. So I went off to his class – some fifth year or other, while I was still in year one or two. He said: 'I didn't tell you to leave!' All these fifth formers started laughing at me as I stood there.

'I thought I ought to go to class,' I said.

'I didn't ask you to think – just do as you're told!'

He embarrassed me and put me down in front of all those kids, and if I saw him in the street today I'd tell him what I think of him. Some teachers were hard on me and I can understand why, but what he did was unnecessary. Teachers who bully you because they can are the lowest of the low. I like to think I'm not that kind of person, someone who picks on people because I can. If I pick on anybody it's the biggest fella, not the littlest one.

I never bunked off school because I was too scared of what my parents would do if they found out. I was absolutely petrified of my dad, Robert, and my mum, Janice. They were in charge and you did what they told you. I rarely, if ever, crossed my mum or my dad. My dad doesn't have a rugby mentality. He never played the game and didn't understand it. He's not a drinker or a Jack-the-lad, though he is small and has a very short fuse. I can remember fighting someone out on the village green one day, how he came out with a horse whip and told us to stop or else! On the whole he is a calm person. His temper is like mine. Probably, he regrets what he's done as soon as he's done it. My dad would always fetch and carry me everywhere. As I got older, he'd pick me up at 11.30 p.m. or so if I'd been out drinking. One night there had been some bother and a guy had hit me with a bottle. I got to the car with this cut on my head and the old man immediately thought it was my fault. The next day he got me up at eight and made me mow the lawns to teach me a lesson. If he said 'Do it!', I did it. He wouldn't let me get away with anything on the rugby pitch either. In one U16 game, the opposing hooker tried to strike for our ball and I shouted 'Kick his f***ing head off!' or something equally mindless. My dad was on the touchline, heard it and gave me a right bollocking afterwards. Not being a rugby man, it was very difficult for him to give me the kind of advice I needed. All he ever said to me was: 'Do your best. If you're good enough you'll be picked.' I still hold that view today, even at the highest level with England. I'm disappointed if I'm left out but there are other things in life. I'm single-minded in what I want to do but if I don't achieve a certain goal and I've given it my best shot, I take a realistic attitude towards it. Some players can be suicidal if they're not picked for a side or a tour.

Nor am I surprised that my mum lost her temper with us now and again. She worked full time, had to cook, clean and wash, and would come home to be asked, 'What's for dinner?' No wonder we got the odd whack round the head – I can remember feeling her wedding ring on my ear more than once! It may be an old-fashioned thing to say these days, but it's not done me any harm, has it? A good clip round the ear was probably the only thing that made me stop and take notice of what was being said to me.

I've got to be honest and admit that as a teenager I was a yob. I was the typical Brit-abroad type of lad: short hair, stocky, drinks loads of beer, behaves how he wants to. I don't think I'm the sort of person who would have got into crime because I'm too frightened of authority, but every Saturday night there would be a spot of bother. I'd do whatever I wanted. Didn't matter whether they were a bouncer in a club or people on the street, I was always up for it after I joined Newbold Rugby Club. The rugby club is the community in Newbold because it is such a small village. My brother joined first so, of course, I had to follow in his footsteps, didn't I? They were great people at Newbold, very loyal, fantastic people. It's not a wealthy area. It's a hard community and we had quite a reputation as a rugby club. We were proud to wear our club tie round the town on a Saturday night and everyone would avoid us like the plague. We'd run amok, though personally I was always lucky with the police. I never had any run-ins with them – more thanks to luck than judgement! There were frequent brawls on the taxi rank in the days before they introduced CCTV. We'd just push in at two or three in the morning and everything would suddenly go a bit pear-shaped!

I'd begun my rugby career at Harris C of E as a loose-head prop. Then I played for Newbold Colts and Newbold U19s – at the age of 15 – as a hooker when they were short one day. There were trials for Rugby town and Warwickshire at U16 and I got in. I made the Midlands squad. I was doing weights and taking things a bit more seriously, thinking to myself, 'I'm quite good at this.' I made the England U16 team. It was an absolutely amazing feeling. I just wanted to be the best I could at the thing I did and so I began to take a lot of pride in my rugby from that moment on.

Playing for Newbold U19s at such a young age was tremendous for me. The challenge of competing against older, bigger, supposedly better players appealed to me for some reason. Other people thought I was an absolute madman, because there would be the biggest guy on the pitch, 6ft 5ins, 18 stone or whatever, and this young, small kid would be there, giving it what I could give. I can recall one of my earliest games at this stage when a lad got hold of my collar and then pinned me to the ground, with his fists raised ready to thump me, and I said: 'Why not get on with it? Do it! I don't care.' I don't know why I'm like that at all but for some reason, if there's a challenge, I'm always in the middle of it doing something or other about it.

After I'd played for England U16 I began training with Coventry. A guy called Don Varden, who had a number-one hit record way back with 'Indian Reservation', ran a pub near us, the Plough at Eathorpe, and he used to cook the food at Coventry. So he began taking me over for training. They had some good players then, such as Graham Robbins, Steve Thomas, Lee Johnson; Andy Farrington was the hooker and Martin Fairn, the full-back, was the captain. At training they scrummaged until they couldn't scrummage any more. They were a very forwards-oriented side. Coventry, as a town, was a rough place generally, so you were playing with tough, hard fellas, likeable rogues. It rubbed off on me.

I was really glad to be there. The Colts often trained alongside the first team and I was always making a pest of myself getting amongst the senior players. I was certainly no star and didn't progress straight into the first XV. During my second season I did get to sit on the bench and eventually got on. I forced my way into the Midlands Colts squad and won the divisional championship with Warwickshire Colts in 1991. Coventry were very reluctant to put youngsters in the firsts. Consequently, no great rivalry ever existed between Andy Farrington and me. I merely wondered whether I'd be good enough for first-team rugby. It's only when you get into the firsts (which I did during 1991–92) that you get noticed, so no one ever said anything to me about toning down my abrasive attitude. In point of fact, I've never been sent off in 'proper' rugby. I was high-tackled in a house match at school; I retaliated and got my marching orders. By now, Leicester were beginning to show an interest in me. I'd been on the bench when Coventry played Leicester in 1991 and had come on as a back-row replacement. Johnno and Backy were playing. Anyway, I was eager to better myself. It was quite a wrench to leave Coventry in the summer of 1992 but I wanted to play with, and against, the big boys.

Up until then I'd been learning as I went along. Nobody really showed me the ropes. As a kid playing against older people you learned pretty quickly or you didn't survive. They'd try to intimidate you, of course. In some of those early local derbies at Newbold, for example, I can remember crying because I'd been whacked. You must live and learn. You can't teach someone how to play in the front row. You must go and do it; play, get stuffed occasionally, get beaten up occasionally, and learn the various tricks of the trade. You gradually acquire the mentality for playing in the front row, which is not a particularly pleasant place to play. After a couple of years it soon becomes second nature. That's why front rows have their own fraternity. It's a completely different world. You can be taught the technical aspects – though I wasn't, particularly – but the learning process is a gradual one. I did have the odd bit of coaching at Coventry from Steve Brain, the England hooker. I was finding it difficult to hook the ball when the scrum went low. I was ending up with my feet underneath my chest and being bent double. I was always keen to learn and never too proud to ask. Brain simply told me that the lower the scrum goes, the further back I should put my feet. A small tip, maybe, but little bits of advice like that accumulate as you develop your play with age and experience. Now, I'm probably technically the best hooker in the country, which affords me enormous pride. You can't learn from a book. You can't learn from coaching. You learn from playing.

Now that I was playing serious rugby I stopped going out on a Friday night with my Newbold mates. I desperately wanted to play well. Even after Saturday's game I'd go home with a couple of bottles of Newcastle Brown, watch *Match of the Day*, and stay out of trouble. That's the sacrifice I made because I wanted to play rugby at a higher level.

Rugby had given me a purpose in life.

THREE

LETTING OFF STEAM

I get a lot of questions from the lads in junior clubs as to whether we still have a drink. In the old days, having a few 'scoops' after the game was your reward because we were not paid. Nowadays, of course, we are professionals and must behave like professionals, so the opportunities are fewer and further between. But you know that whenever there's a night out at Leicester, certain guys will be there – the front row, me, Darren Garforth and Graham Rowntree; Neil Back, Dorian West and Johnno; and the young fellas like Lewis Moody and Paul Gustard. The guys who have played junior rugby seem to know more about the *craic* than those who have only ever played professional rugby. Too many of the boys these days have gone from school to university and then straight into the professional game. They've probably never even played junior rugby and have no idea what the game really means at that level. When I was playing Colts rugby at Newbold, for instance, it was just an excuse to get away into town on a Saturday night, go on the piss with my mates and look for birds. Nobody took the rugby very seriously at that stage – it's social rugby. The playing and the winning are secondary to the enjoyment. I'm always getting guys coming up to me bemoaning the fact that they only play junior rugby and they're missing out on something as a result. I tell them to forget it, because the game is all about enjoying yourself and not the level at which you play.

We are never afraid to let our hair down at Leicester. On the bus coming back from a game, for example, Daz Garforth and Westy will lead the singing, usually the customary filthy rugby songs; there'll be a few videos of the dubious variety and the beer will flow. When I speak to other clubs on the subject, they can't believe what we get up to. It's the mentality we've always had at Leicester. It helps to form that priceless bond, so you know when things get tough on the pitch the guys will be there for you.

The night of the 1996 Pilkington Cup final, which we lost 15–16 to Bath, when Steve Lander awarded a late penalty try against us, was a cracker. There was no dinner or anything like that at Twickenham after the game. We were due back in Leicester for a 'do', at the Holiday Inn, I think. We'd hardly got out of Twickenham proper before we stopped at an off-licence. We loaded up with beer and, fatally, bottles of port. Everyone was bitterly disappointed with the outcome of the game. We felt we'd been robbed. Our sorrows had to be drowned. It didn't take long for things to start getting out of hand. I was more uncontrollable than I am now. We had been supplied by Next with all this sponsored kit, suits, shirts and ties, all very up-market gear. Pretty soon I'm leaning over people to rip the breast pocket off their shirt. Well, here we go, isn't it? Someone does it to me. Then it's collars. And a fight for the back seat – a massive punch-up in the back of the bus! Rory Underwood was sitting at the front of the bus reading a newspaper – a legend in his own lifetime who doesn't drink –

so I went up to him, grabbed the paper, tore it to shreds and then proceeded to rip off his collar. Eventually, all the shirts and ties were thrown out of the skylight and our trousers were in tatters. Westy, who didn't even play, had to have four stitches in his leg through getting rammed up against the metal leg of a table. Even the coaches, Dodgy and Dosser – Paul Dodge and Ian Smith – were brawling.

All the wives and girlfriends had gone back to Leicester on a separate coach and were waiting for us at the hotel. You can imagine the reception we got when we turned up battered and bruised and dressed in rags. The mayor was waiting to greet us and you should have seen his face! We went upstairs to get changed for the function and it all kicked off again. The girls soon walked out on us and went to bed early and a few of us began lobbing plates across the room, smashing them against the wall. Deano came into the room with a bread basket on his head and a tablecloth round his shoulders, carrying a fire extinguisher and calling himself 'Tablecloth Man' and started spraying everyone. Glasses were now being used for ammunition. We were throwing anything and everything at each other. We were destroying the place, yet the management didn't appear to mind. We asked for another six bottles of red wine, for instance, and thought they'd say 'No chance!'. Next thing, the wine arrives! I've no idea who paid for it all. I wound up sitting in the foyer next to a big glass coffee table covered with empty glasses. I began sticking my foot underneath it, gradually lifting it up until all the glasses slid off and shattered. Mindless vandalism, really – a typical rugby night out! You couldn't do it these days but back then the free booze was our reward for playing and the outrageous behaviour was more tolerated.

Whenever high jinks off the field are talked about, sooner or later the Barbarians crop up in the conversation. The Baa-baas are a bit more laid-back than other sides so it's always fun playing for them. You don't have the pressure in the build-up that you have in an international. Obviously, it's deadly serious on match day but either side of kick-off everything is in good spirits. To be picked to play for such a world-famous club is a great achievement; it's good for your portfolio as a rugby player if people see you are good enough to play for the Barbarians. They are an invitation side which draws players from all over the world, and every world-class player harbours ambitions to play for them. To be considered in the same category as the numerous legends who have represented the Barbarians is a fantastic feeling. Ask anyone around the world about the Barbarians and they'll all say the same thing. I've got two Barbarians shirts at home. You receive them only if you play in a Test, and I'm very happy to have been involved. I've been invited to play since I've been capped and it still ranks as a tremendous honour.

My first experience of the Barbarians came from playing against them for Leicester in the traditional fixture over Christmas. For a lot of the Leicester guys in the amateur days it was the biggest game of the season. The post-match dinners were always special. I can recall one, at the Grand, I think, when we'd drunk so much beer that we started throwing ice cubes around – especially towards the top table where, once again, the poor old mayor was sitting. One ice cube landed right in his glass and smashed it! I don't think he was very impressed. John Allen, the club's honorary secretary at the time, came over to our table to administer a bollocking and tell us to calm down. He walked off and Daz threw a lump of ice in his general direction and it hit him right on top of his head – and 'Gubby' is somewhat bald! The whole place erupted. There were large bottles of fizzy water on each table and Peter Wheeler shook a two-litre bottle, undid the cap and threw it at us. He was worse than we were! When the complaints began arriving a few days later, our defence was that the committee men were more badly behaved than the players.

When you are representing the Barbarians you tend to be better behaved than when you're with your club because you want to make a good impression. Even so, your defences drop on occasions. From personal experience I can say that a tour to Zimbabwe with the Baa-baas and a trip to Dublin for the Peace International of 1996 were particularly eventful.

The Zimbabwe tour of 1994 was the first time I played for the Barbarians. At the time I wasn't capped, so it was my greatest honour in the game. I think they were short of numbers after a few people were forced to drop out and Micky Steele-Bodger rang me. I think Micky and Geoff Windsor Lewis, the other Baa-baas selector, had doubts about whether I was a Barbarian sort of player because of the way I performed at times as a youngster. Micky said: 'We'd like you to come to Zimbabwe if you promise to behave yourself.' Micky Steele-Bodger is a great bloke who embodies the attitude all rugby players should have. He wants you to enjoy yourself – which is not a bad philosophy. Anyway, I had to promise him over the phone that I'd be a good boy. And I was – up to a point.

The trip was more like a holiday than a rugby tour. Nigel Meek, the Welsh hooker, and Aled Williams, the Swansea fly-half, were fantastic singers and used to lead that side of things. The matches were taken very seriously, naturally, but once training was over things could get out of hand. We tended to train in these sort of colonial clubs, with polo pitches and everything. The problem was that it would get so hot later in the day that we had to train at nine in the morning. One morning, six of us – Derwyn Jones, Aled Williams, the other Welsh fly-half Colin Stephens, Derek Eves the Bristol flanker, Daz Garforth and me – decided to stay on afterwards for a drink. The booze was ridiculously cheap. We're downing double gin and tonics at ten in the morning. We don't feel like leaving. More G-and-Ts. Some tackle shields are discovered at one end of the veranda, in front of the clubhouse, so we begin running the length of the place, crashing into them at full pelt. A bloke comes out and orders us to stop. Our reply is to rifle him into the tackle shields! Daz, Eves and I strike up the national anthem and the abuse really starts. It increases during a series of 'boat races'. One local in particular is giving us grief, standing at the bar. I hurl my half-pint glass at him and it whistles past his head and shatters on the bar, missing him by inches. At this, another drinker at the bar comes across and flicks his fag-end, still alight, in my face – but before I can get my first punch in, Daz has levelled him. That was the signal for us to be chucked out. We'd been in there from ten in the morning till eight or nine o'clock at night!

Two years later, Daz, Graham Rowntree, Deano and I were invited to play for the Baa-baas in the Peace International against Ireland, which was in aid of the victims of the Troubles. This was a big deal for us because, although everyone knew Dean, and Graham was capped, no one really knew me or Daz. We were to meet at the Dublin hotel at ten o'clock on the Thursday, the game being on Saturday. We got there early and Jim Hay, a Scottish hooker, said the afternoon's training session had been cancelled because all the foreign contingent were going to be late arriving.

We decided to go into town for some lunch and a drink. We started with a couple of orange juices, all very proper, but eventually thought better of it and decided we might as well have a Guinness. By 1 p.m. we must have sunk six or seven pints of Guinness and were well on our way to being pretty pissed. We decided to try another bar. The barman took one look at us and said: 'We don't serve groups of lads.' The bar happened to have three different doors to it, so we went outside and walked back in through the three separate doors and he said: 'No problem!' By this stage I was becoming uncontrollable. I'd got a bit of a cold and felt I needed to clear my throat on to the floor. That did get us thrown out!

As we tumbled out onto the pavement, a double-decker bus pulled up. We instinctively got on it, even though we hadn't a clue where it was going. It was nearly three o'clock and it turned out that the bus was full of schoolkids. Well, Daz always has trouble with 'wind' and, sure enough, he dropped his guts before we'd gone half a mile. All these poor kids were holding their noses and groaning. We eased their suffering by getting off the bus and stumbling into the nearest wine bar, full of business types. Some-one fancied a cigar, so we smoked those and drank Baileys as an accompaniment. The bar rapidly emptied as we were so obnoxious!

At around 4.30 p.m. we return to the hotel to check out what's happening, only to find Micky Steele-Bodger standing in the lobby waiting for us. 'We're training! All the boys have turned up. We're training in ten minutes! The bus is waiting!' We are all absolutely twisted. We get on the bus 20 minutes late. Everyone knows Dean, but Daz and I are just men from Mars as far as these guys are concerned. These world-famous figures – Campese,

Joubert, Pienaar, Cabannes, Mike Brewer, Eric Rush – are gob-smacked. They can only stare as we shamble onto the bus. The training was at Blackrock College, quite an event for the kids being able to watch the Barbarians train. There are almost five hundred kids waiting for us. We do some stride-outs before the team-run and Graham falls flat on his face, half-unconscious, he's so pissed. He just lies there, laughing hysterically, until we drag him upright again. We manage to survive until it's time for lineout practice. Daz and Graham have to lift Brouzet, this huge French lock. The first throw I take goes yards over his head and Wig, instead of lifting him by the shorts, mistakenly lifts him by the shirt – and it goes right over Brouzet's head so he can't see! The rest look on incredulously. Dean is meant to be in charge of the forwards and he thinks it's all hilarious. He says: 'We'll forget the front then, and throw some to Cabannes at the back.' Now, Cabannes is supposed to run ten yards backwards and I'm supposed to hit him. The only problem is I can hardly see him by this time. I can't even manage to get the ball to him, let alone get it straight. It was absolute chaos. We finished with some scrums and I threw up. I dread to think what everyone thought of this lunatic Leicester front row! The following day we trained in the morning before being taken to the Guinness brewery for lunch – not an ideal preparation for a big match – but we did go on to hammer Ireland on the day.

Touring, or staying away overnight for that matter, is fraught with danger. You never leave the door to your room open or you can expect something to get robbed. In Australia last year everyone had two keys to their room. Wig, aka Graham Rowntree, was foolish enough to leave one of them on his table, so I pocketed it. On the Saturday night after we'd had a few scoops, I let myself into his room before he got back, rolled back his bed covers, took the free coffee from the table and emptied all the granules over the sheets. I topped it off with a covering of beer. It made a lovely brown, shitty coating! Utterly childish, I know, but that's the sort of caper you must watch out for.

Not that you're safe back in Leicester. Matt Poole has always had nice cars. Once he got himself a Nissan convertible and made the mistake of leaving a brand new set of golf clubs on the front seat – with the roof down. Daz nicked them, put them in his car and drove off. Pooley got them back a week later. He had to bite the bullet. You must never leave yourself open. Never leave your food on the table after training because you'll come back to find it plastered with pepper or salt. You forget your towel – you use someone else's and then put it back in his bag. Recently, Daz's missus bought him a load of new underwear from Marks and Spencer. Wig and I are forever nicking his clean underwear from his bag while he's in the shower, and we made off with this lot. The next Daz sees of his underpants is me and Wig wearing them at the next training session. 'I've got some like that,' he says before the two of us start giggling and give the game away.

Everyone gets caught out eventually, everyone gets their turn. I've had my passport nicked at the airport, for instance. You're usually left at the check-in looking a complete prat with the airline staff scratching their heads and wondering what to do. It'll be returned but you're made to sweat. The more fuss you make the worse it gets. Eric Miller, for example, couldn't cope with the piss being taken out of him while he was at Leicester and, in a way, it broke him. But in a rugby environment, if you can't laugh at yourself you won't survive. If you just turn up every day, train and go home, it would be dead boring, wouldn't it?

Women aren't much of a problem these days. Once upon a time most clubhouses tended to be frequented by a number of regulars – rugby groupies, I suppose you'd call them. Those days seem to have gone. You still get a few on tour but it's only the single lads who indulge. They're out to enjoy themselves, so why not? The married guys behave themselves. The majority miss home more than anything. And these days, with the press being the way they are, you can get stitched up very easily. If you're away working and your wife is at home waiting for you to come back, you just have to hope she's behaving as well as you are, don't you? It's all a matter of trust. Enforced celibacy is a problem on tour, but there's always a supply of magazines and videos which you can look at to keep yourself entertained. A lot of the guys do receive letters from girls but you can't help thinking that they, along with the ones who might follow you around, are not likely to be too mentally stable. You want to avoid them like the plague. Backy gets a few letters from teenage girls, and so does Johnno. They ignore them on the whole because you can't risk putting yourself in a compromising situation. You'd end up embarrassing yourself and the club. I've been pretty trouble-free. The reason for that is ever so simple: most of my fans are little girls and old ladies!

FOUR

ALL FOR ONE AND
ONE FOR ALL

TEAM spirit comes from mutual respect. I've played with guys, even at Leicester, whom I don't particularly like, but on the rugby pitch, because they're good players and they work hard, I can respect them and accept them for what they are. If a guy is doing a good job, you don't have to like him. You can make allowances. I'm sure there are people at Leicester who think I'm a bit over the top and too full of myself, and yet because I do what I do quite well, they respect me for that and accept that it's just the way I am. We all share that kind of philosophy at Leicester, and it's not just confined to the forwards either. Guys like Stuart Potter and Leon Lloyd are the same – even Austin Healey to a certain point.

Austin came to Leicester in 1996 with some baggage, a reputation for being a pain. The famous quote about him was attributed to the press officer of his previous club, Orrell, who said something to the effect that he would be better off kept in a cage all week and only allowed out between 3 and 4 p.m. on a Saturday.

A bit harsh, perhaps, but you can appreciate where the Orrell guy was coming from.

Austin and I have had our disagreements. One set-to happened in Italy in October 1997 after we'd beaten Milan in the European Cup. The Milan people presented me with a big trophy for being the Man of the Match. They were taking the piss, really. Anyway, back at the hotel we had a few bottles of red wine and began taking it to bits – it was only bolted together. It must have been about two in the morning when Austin got back to the hotel, and he was in one of his gobshite moods. He's a whole lot better nowadays but then, during his second season at the club, he could be a right pain in the arse. He and Will Greenwood were both completely bladdered. They started taking the piss out of me, which was okay, but Austin started kicking this cup about. Then Greenwood joined in. So I slapped him across the face with the back of my hand. Austin said, 'Don't hit my mate,' and came towards me, a bit aggressively, so I gave him a right hook in the face. 'What did you do that for?' he said.

He needed taking down a peg or two. 'Nobody likes you! F★★★ off!' I told him and, turning to Greenwood, I went on: 'And you can f★★★ off back to Harlequins as well! We're Leicester boys here!' Austin took a run at me and I dumped him on his back on this marble floor. By now the desk clerk was threatening to call the police. I wasn't going to risk getting involved with the police – so I told Austin that I was off to bed. He came at me again and I pushed him away, telling him that I was getting out before the police arrived. Austin was going berserk and shouted – and I couldn't help laughing at his words – 'I don't care, I'll go down for it!'

Austin's toed the line a little since then. Now he's a pretty good fella. He's learned that he doesn't have to prove himself all the time. And he can play, and he does play for the team. I can remember being under the cosh down in Toulouse in a European Cup game. We were only a couple of points ahead when their winger made a break and looked odds on to score. Out of nowhere, Austin steamed across to make this fantastic cover tackle in the corner. Whatever you think of him, and on occasions he can be a right big-headed gobshite, at that moment on that day he stuck his body on the line for the team and won the game for us. I'd never tell him that – but if he hadn't made that tackle we'd have lost. Mind you, there were lots of other things in the game which, had we not done them, would have cost us the game. But Austin didn't have to do what he did. Even if you don't like him you have to respect him for doing what he did. He's a loose cannon, yes, but he cared so much for the team that he was prepared to give his all for it. Because of the way he is, people tend to lose sight of all the good things he does and all the good things he has in him. Austin possesses a lot of qualities but it's easier for people to look at the bad bits.

Austin has won our respect as a player. So-called bonding sessions – nights out go-karting or whatever – are all very well and good but the crux of the matter is that if you're playing with a guy, you want to know that when the shit hits the fan he'll be right behind you, looking after your back. On the pitch, this might mean your team-mate leathers someone from the opposition who is taking the opportunity to get stuck into you or has landed a cheap shot on you. Some guys will stand back and not get involved. No matter how good they might be as a player, I find it very hard to respect someone who behaves like that. That's not the Leicester way. You start on one of our forwards and you've got another seven to contend with straightaway. That's one of Leicester's strengths and always has been. Mess with one of us and you've got a whole lot of trouble coming your way. That's always been the Leicester way. We had a mighty brawl with Sale at Welford Road one year. Deano was whacking somebody. Now, you are liable to get yourself into a spot of bother if you start running into things from some distance away. If you're there when the punch-up begins you're okay, but if you run ten to fifteen yards in order to join in, that spells trouble. So, Deano is hitting this number 8 of Sale and another one of them comes up behind him, grabbing him so that the number 8 is able to land a few blows on Dean. I'm a good ten yards away. I thought, 'I can't let this happen but if I steam in from here I'm heading for trouble.' You think on your feet in those situations. The options are simple. You let your mate get duffed up or you take the risk of being sent off. I went in fists first. That's all you can do, really. That's why the Leicester pack has been so strong and so feared. One in, all in!

Another example involved Martin Corry in a game against Northampton in 1998. Off the pitch, Cozza's got the biggest conscience in the world. He'd never do anybody any harm. In this particular game versus the Saints at Welford Road, Backy and Tim Rodber were having a dig at each other, so Cozza comes in and drops Rodders with a short elbow in the face. One of their second row then butts in to sort out Cozza, who promptly drops him on his arse with a big right hook. Off Cozza went for that one. It was Martin's first season with the club, but within four or five months of being at Leicester we'd instilled that sort of response and team unity into him. Had he stood off and let it all happen in front of him, allowed Backy to take a hammering, he would have lost our respect. Consequently, he earned a load of brownie points from the boys for stepping in like he did. He'd risked getting sent off to look after one of his mates. That's what team spirit is all about. We look out for each other.

Occasionally moments arise during a season when you realise just how tightly the team has bonded. One such defining moment during our Premiership success of 1998–99 came at Richmond. We'd had a few injuries, especially among the backs, and midweek fixtures away from home seldom see us at our best. Richmond were good, yet we still beat them 23–11. They battered our line for 20 minutes but everyone stood up to be counted, everyone from number 1 to number 15. Scrummaging, lineouts, tackling; the backs sticking their heads in where they really shouldn't; Dave Lougheed knocking lumps out of opponents; Patty Howard getting kicked about. After a victory like that you do become very tightly knit. From then on we believed we could win the league. We developed a real mental toughness. The following week London Irish visited Welford Road. They were enjoying a successful streak. They need not have bothered turning up. We battered them into submission 31–10. It was no contest. We could have capitulated at Richmond, conceded a couple of soft tries and lost the game as the pressure increased. Our season could have begun to disintegrate as a result, with London Irish being the first to benefit. We didn't allow that to happen, and team spirit had a lot to do with it.

Funnily enough, we'd also excelled ourselves against Richmond at home. Will Greenwood was injured, Joel Stransky was out and Pots was injured. Jim Overend and Jon Stuart – two young lads, good players but new to it – played in the centre. We went out there and trounced Richmond, with all the young players excelling themselves – they were the difference, not all the so-called big names. That was the story of the season, with guys like Jon Stuart, Jim Overend, Geordon Murphy and so on, coming in for the established names and doing the business for the club. In the Deano era you always wondered how you were going to win if he didn't play. Nowadays it doesn't matter if a first-teamer is out injured. We'd got to the stage where it doesn't matter who plays. We never gave it a second thought. If Joel was out we knew that Pat Howard at fly-half and Jon Stuart and Jim Overend in the centre were all tough, uncompromising players who'd do the job without any problem.

Moments of team bonding can materialise in defeat, too – it doesn't have to be via success. Take that Pilkington Cup final loss to Bath when Steve Lander awarded that penalty try which cost us the match. Backy refused to go and get his loser's mug; so did John Wells – he called the ref a f***ing tosser. There were lots of senior players in the team who thought they'd never get another chance. Tears were plentiful. I tried to gee people up, saying 'People have paid good money to come and support us – let's be proud of what we've achieved. Heads up, chests out!' – that sort of thing, but it cut no ice. I did go up to get my runners-up mug, but I threw it straight in the bin as soon as I got back into the changing-room because I felt we had been robbed of victory. Deano took his glass tankard out of the box and hurled it as hard as he could against the wall. One of my most vivid memories of that game is the sight of Dosser Smith, one of our coaches, sweeping all the glass off the floor from those broken mugs. The newspapers said that Leicester were bad sports because they didn't even keep their trophies. To me that kind of stuff was a load of bollocks because it's *my* trophy, *I* earned it and I could do what I liked with it. I didn't want to keep the damn thing because we didn't deserve to have the losers' trophy that day, we deserved to win. To see people like Deano and Wellsy almost in tears on account of it was terribly hard to take. It was a difficult time for all of us. But the crucial point I want to make is that setbacks like this can bring you together. A team can muster some sort of inner strength out of adversity. We returned the following year to beat Sale 9–3 and win the cup for real.

The training ground is another source of team spirit. At Leicester we don't tend to give new signings any respect, regardless of how big a name they are, until we see them perform for the club. We don't treat 'stars' with kid gloves at Leicester. They receive as much stick and banter as everyone else. I think it's important that they're here to play for the team rather than for themselves, and they must realise that from the outset. When Joel Stransky first appeared, for example, we were training in the indoor arena at Worcester – because the pitches were frozen – in preparation for the semi-final of the European Cup against Toulouse. Joel came dressed in jeans and a T-shirt and was kicking a ball around by himself. Bob Dwyer introduced him to us and I said to Joel: 'I've got some kit in the car if you want to do some training. You don't want to stand around watching, mate.' You don't want to put someone on a pedestal, whoever they happen to be. Everyone respected Joel for what he did in the World Cup for South Africa but you need to get some banter going pretty quickly, and a new guy has to prove himself all over again when he comes to Leicester.

It was the same with Waisale Serevi. We all knew he was a fantastic sevens player, a real legend on the sevens circuit. However, no one thought he was a good fifteens player. I'd never ever met him before he turned up to our pre-season training camp in

Limerick prior to the 1997–98 Premiership. Someone collected him from the airport and this strange sight met our eyes. It was pissing down with rain, freezing cold, and Serevi walks in wrapped up to the eyeballs in this huge overcoat. You could hardly see his face. It was as if he thought he was going to Antarctica! Waisale was a really humble guy. He'd just come from Japan and whenever he came into a room or bumped into you somewhere, he'd execute this sort of half-bow, like the Japanese do. So we started returning it, with our hands together, as in prayer. Also, every time he spoke in Fijian I fined him a pound – because I was in charge of fines on the trip. We had a couple of wigs, too, which had to be worn by anyone who swore too much or lost their sense of humour, and we got Waisale to wear one once or twice. The sight of this tiny black fella with a red wig on was hilarious. It was all in good fun – which he appreciated – and made him feel welcome. He couldn't stop laughing the entire week we were in Ireland, and it was no different once we got back to Leicester. He'd run rings round us playing 'touch' at Oval Park and you'd say: 'Wizza, do that again and I'll kick your head in!' He'd run off laughing and promptly do it again. He was a fantastic guy to have around.

One night there was a 'gentlemen's evening' over at Newbold. A few of the lads went across and I invited Waisale. He really enjoyed himself and they loved him in return. The Newbold boys were used to seeing the likes of Johnno around Leicester, but to see a living legend from the South Pacific at a small junior club in Rugby was fantastic for them. He was so kind-hearted and would do anything for anybody. A Japanese firm sponsored his boots, for instance. I asked him why he didn't switch to Nike or Adidas because they'd pay a fortune to sign up someone like him. He told me that this Japanese firm supplied all the kit for his local team back home in Fiji as part of the deal and he felt obliged to help them. Waisale was a really genuine bloke and even though things went a bit sour for him towards the end, after Bob Dwyer left, I was truly disappointed to see him go.

Some of the things Waisale did reduced us to tears of laughter on more than one occasion. After he hurt his knee one time, the doc told him to have two or three days off training. He should have come in for treatment but he took the doc's words quite literally and no one saw him for three days. He just stayed at home. One time, we had some days off and Waisale went back to Fiji to see his family – and didn't even bother to lock his front door. He lived in a farmhouse and by the time he returned the chickens from the farm had made their home in his kitchen. It never entered his mind to lock up the place because in Fiji he's such a god nobody would ever do anything to upset him.

The time he really brought the house down was after we'd beaten Toulouse 22–17, in Toulouse, in the European Cup. As you can imagine, it was somewhat raucous on the coach going back to the hotel. Everyone was getting up, singing a song or doing their party piece. Up goes the cry, 'Wizza, Wizza, give us a song!' and Waisale goes to the front of the bus, picks up the microphone and begins this song, in Fijian of course. It was totally incomprehensible to us. Anyway, he stops and everyone applauds, thinking he'd finished. But he hadn't. It was only the first verse. Waisale just kept staring out the front window, singing verse after verse for what seemed an eternity! The whole bus was in hysterics. When he eventually finished we gave him a rapturous round of applause. He'd made the effort to join in, you see. We respect that. It's how team spirit develops.

It's not all sweetness and light at our training ground, Oval Park.

If things kick off in training, they really kick off! Some coaches encourage it. The odd bout of fisticuffs is not necessarily a bad thing. I've certainly had a few set-tos with my Leicester understudy, Dorian West. When Westy first came back to Leicester from Nottingham there was a session where we were doing contact of some description and I'd been knocked to the floor. As Westy went past me, I booted him right on the shins, as hard as I could. 'You yellow-bellied bastard!' he shouted. Then, at a scrum, it got a bit heated. Westy and Deano are good mates – they were both in the police – and Deano was watching, so I think West was trying to impress him. Anyway, we went into this scrum and Daz came across Westy and dropped the swede on him – gave him a head butt – causing the scrum to disintegrate with all hell breaking loose. West stood there yelling at me: 'I'm not scared of you, you know!' I just had to laugh. In actual fact, Westy is a great character and a good player. On the field we're never going to get on because we're rivals – if we get a chance we'll have a dig at each other, no question. He's very, very talented, very quick – he is a converted flanker – and possesses a good rugby brain, but I wonder whether he has the desire to push himself enough in order to play top-class rugby consistently at club and international level. I've always been hungrier than Westy. My attitude has always been better, I feel. I want to play every week, whereas Westy is happy to sit on the bench and play here and there, which wouldn't suit me – my competitiveness won't allow it. I tend to be rested for the 'easy' games, which gives Westy the chance to shine. This helped him get a couple of caps as a replacement. I don't begrudge him his two caps – far from it, he deserved them. But he hasn't pushed himself to stay involved at that level, which is a pity because you get only one bite at the cherry. The easy part is getting there, the hardest part is staying there. Socially, Westy is a great fella and we get on fine. Off the pitch you have to put all rivalry aside.

Bust-ups in training, then, do happen, and I've been involved, not altogether surprisingly, in a fair few. One such involved a flanker of ours called Dick Beaty. We were getting match fit early in the season and were playing against the second XV. These sort of 'games' in training are never refereed in the proper sense of the word. Things go on that can never happen on a Saturday: you get offside; hold onto the ball on the floor; kill the ball, and so on. Naturally, it's the seconds who tend to pull these strokes. The next thing you know, the coach starts bollocking the firsts, 'Why's the ball not coming back properly? They're only the seconds – what's the matter with you?' The temperature begins to rise then, doesn't it? Things become a lot more physical, and if someone comes round the wrong side, they are trodden on or whacked. With no proper referee, you have to do something about it yourself. Well, Dick Beaty was a pretty good open-side flanker who'd played in New Zealand, but he was one of those guys forever killing the ball. We had been taught to clear players who did this off the ball by coming in low and using your forearm to lift them up and away. I gave him one dig and told him not to do it again. He looked at me and kind of said: 'So what?' He did it again. I cleared him away in the accepted manner but my forearm cracked his cheekbone. I apologised to him in the physio's room afterwards and he seemed all right about it. He must have had second thoughts later on because solicitors became involved. I had to attend a disciplinary hearing at the club. I contended that, although the intention had been to get rid of him from our side of the ball and cause him some grief for being such a pain in the arse, his injury was purely accidental. It was all quite worrying, as only a few months earlier Simon Devereux of Gloucester had been sentenced to nine months' imprisonment for doing something similar in a game. The club found me not guilty through lack of evidence, and that finding remains on my record. If I have any more disciplinary hearings, it will be taken into account. I think Dick Beaty knows it was an accident. These things do happen and I've been on the receiving end plenty of times myself. I wouldn't have wished such an injury on anybody.

Three or four weeks after that incident on the training pitch, I got myself into another scrape during some routine contact drills: one guy with the ball runs into three others dressed in tackle suits and has to play the ball back – a skill to develop your reactions in a situation where you become isolated or outnumbered. Daz takes the ball into contact, where Gary Becconsall, one of our scrum-halves, was on one end of the three defenders. Daz was having trouble getting the ball back, so I thought I'd run in and clear one side of the ball for him – which I wasn't meant to do. I run in and whack Gary Becconsall, who falls backwards onto his shoulder and dislocates it. With the Beaty incident still fresh in the mind I'm hardly flavour of the month. Fortunately, Bob Dwyer was in the vicinity and saw what happened. It was another accident, but . . .

I got my comeuppance a month or so later. We were playing 'touch' in training shortly before the European Cup final of 1997 with Brive down in Cardiff. I'd turned to chase Matt Poole for a 'touch', and as I did so I felt someone grab my shirt and pull me back. Without a second thought I swung my arm back and smashed whoever did it right in the chops. Of course, that person had to be Deano, didn't it? He rubbed his jaw for a moment and then he grabbed me by the scruff of the neck and started laying into me. He was punching me and I was trying to avoid his fists because he's not exactly the weakest of men. A few blows were traded but I can assure you the vast majority of them landed on one place – the top of my head. You mix it with Deano at your peril.

FIVE

DISHING IT OUT

THEY say violence breeds violence. But I'm not a violent person within society as a whole. I am a violent person on the rugby field. That is the nature of the sport. In society today there has to be an outlet for our aggressive tendencies. We were put on this earth as men and we're hunter-gatherers, aren't we? We're made to go out and hunt and be aggressive. That's the nature of men generally. So where do you allow this aggression to come out? Is it in the pub on a Saturday night, or is it on the rugby field on a Saturday afternoon? Personally, fortunately, I've got an escape clause in my life where I can behave like a lunatic or a man possessed. If more people played sport they could channel their aggressive streak into tackling or kicking a ball – which is prefer-able to going down the pub, drinking a few beers and brawling on the pavement, as I used to do as a youngster.

I'm often asked where rugby's hard men get their aggression from. I think you're born with a hard streak. You can't coach hardness into a player. If anything, hardness is coached *out* of players these days. Kids, and people in general, don't take enough physical exercise. I've got all this energy inside of me that I want to get rid of – be it aggressive energy or nervous energy – and if I don't get rid of it on the rugby field or in the gym or on the training ground, where will all that pent-up aggression go? Do I go to a football match and become a hooligan? Do I go to the pub for a scrap? That's probably what could happen if I didn't play rugby. If you are a competitive person and you like the aggressive side of things, rugby is a fantastic way to utilise that energy. If some kids put all the energy they expend on nicking cars and joyriding into a sport like rugby or boxing or wrestling they'd be much better off. I'm not saying I'd have become a hooligan or a criminal, because I don't think my upbringing would have allowed it, but I would have been involved in more things than I should have. With the mentality I possess – and I do have this element of nastiness in me – I must unload all this aggression somewhere, and that is not always easy to achieve in a safe environment. Rugby provides one such relatively safe place.

Right from the start at Newbold I was taught to give the opposition plenty of stick – physically, verbally, any way. Playing for Newbold was all about physical intimidation. Most junior rugby is no different, and I loved it. We could mix it with the best at Coventry Colts as well. One day we played Moseley Colts and a scuffle erupted, involving me and Joe Garforth, Daz's brother, among others. Joe's dad, Jim, was watching and he came on to the pitch to split us up, whereupon the Moseley number 8 ran over and smacked him one. That was the signal for a mass brawl involving players and spectators. Joe Garforth is a handful at the best of times but once he saw his father being hit, he got hold of this Moseley bloke – who was a big bugger – by the hair and started whacking his head against the wire fence that surrounded the pitch. Anyway, the game eventually resumed and we won. Everyone trooped back down the tunnel, in the middle of the stand, towards the dressing-rooms; ours was on the right and the visitors' on the left. Moseley went in first, as the visitors, and I was following Joe Garforth down the tunnel. We were soulmates, he'd follow me anywhere and I'd follow him, sort of thing. What does Joe do? Instead of turning right into our dressing-room, he turns left and follows Moseley into theirs. I go with him, and see him go straight up to this number 8 and drop a head-butt on him! It all kicks off again in the changing-room. The story even made *The Daily Telegraph* and *The Times*. Joe is a smaller version of Daz, a scaffolder, a rough diamond, salt of the earth. We'd have taken on the world.

I think people have the wrong perception of what a hard man is. Does being hard describe someone who is big and aggressive and not scared of anything *because* they're bigger than everyone else? Or is it the little fella, who may be absolutely shitting himself and still goes in to make that tackle, who is the real hard man? They are two different types. One likes to go around swinging his fists and probably enjoys acquiring a reputation for himself. The other is quiet and unassuming yet will do the business when necessary. You're talking about the truly hard men and the merely nasty – those who go for the cheap shot, squeeze your balls or poke you where they shouldn't. I've played against some who are great at giving it out, fisticuffs or stamping, but as soon as they get some back they squeal like pigs. It's the school-bully syndrome. Once you stand up to them, they tend to back down.

Rugby's hard men are not the guys who go round punching and kicking people: those who do are the cheap-shot, dirty players. The truly hard men are those who get the tackles in and put their heads where it hurts. A prime example of a hard man is John Wells, one of the toughest players you could ever come up against, but I can honestly say I don't think I ever saw him so much as throw a punch in a game. When it came to tackling and getting stuck in, he was second to none. Although he does like his fisticuffs occasionally, Darren Garforth is the same kind of player, always going in where it hurts. Stuart Potter is another unsung hard man. You'd never see Pots fighting, in any circumstances, but on the rugby field, running full tilt at people and knocking them over, he's a top man. Patty Howard, likewise, is almost fearless; Neil Back, one of the smallest men on the field, is the first man to stick his head at the feet of the biggest bloke. That is the correct interpretation of a hard man.

Having said that, any team needs a balance. It needs its fair quota of hard men who go where the sun doesn't shine. It also requires the 'henchmen'. These are the individuals who go in feet and fists first to sort out what the referee can't see – killing the ball, lying over the ball, slowing it down. If you are allowed to kill everything you'll do it again, for sure. If you go over the ball that first occasion and get 16 pieces of aluminium stuck in your back, you're unlikely to do it again. Many sides do possess someone you need to keep an eye on. Mick Watson, who has been with West Hartlepool and 'Quins and later with London Scottish, is a good player but you always know somewhere in the game he'll be in a punch-up, giving it some welly. Dean Ryan, of Wasps, Newcastle and currently Bristol, is another who loves to mix it whenever he can. One man doing it on his own, however, is asking for trouble. He will get sorted, especially if he's foolish enough to do it against Leicester. Try it on with one of us and he'll have to contend with the whole pack.

Anything can spark trouble. Too much abuse, a bit of phlegm in the wrong direction, anything. There is nothing worse for a hooker than going into a scrum with his arms pinned behind his back, and his opposite number spits in his face. You're trapped there with phlegm dribbling down your face and you can't wipe it away. If you go around the park with the attitude I have, you are going to get whacked, no doubt about it. At Bristol one time, I cleared Alan Sharp, the Scottish prop, from the side of a ruck, and as I drove into his midriff he walloped me on the back of the head. Off it went! Hinkins, the other prop, grabbed hold of me and I began to get absolutely pummelled. Blood was pouring from the top of my head. Then all I can remember is a load of bodies arriving and piling in. The video showed Graham Rowntree running in from 20 yards to knock both of them off me. No worries. If you don't get him back later in that game, there's always later in the season or the following season. There's always going to be that time in the future when he's going to be on the floor and you're going to be on your feet. I learned that early on from people like Deano and Wellsy, who would get hold of me when I was ready to chase someone round the field and whack them then and there: 'Don't worry. You'll get your chance.' And that chance does come around. And I've somehow survived. I've still got all my own teeth – and I don't wear a gumshield. No broken nose. No cauliflower ears. Just as beautiful as the day I was born!

There are some things that are really out of order, real crimes that transgress any unofficial code of conduct or code of honour among even the hardest of forwards. Number one is eye gouging, which is totally unacceptable. French club rugby, for instance, seems to be extremely physical and very violent, and from personal experience in France I've no reason to think otherwise.

They are so passionate about the game and will do anything to win. The refereeing standards, I feel, are lower in France than over here and the violence stems from that, because players tend to get away with more than they would anywhere else. They just love their forward confrontation down in the south of France. It's a very male thing, a macho thing. Lots of pride is at stake and their forwards can never be seen to back down or avoid a confrontation. In one sense it's great to go down there to play because you really test the mettle of your team when you visit places like Pau or Toulouse. When all is said and done, though, poking people in the eyes is pretty cowardly. It's almost automatic when you've got the ball in a maul, say, and if you don't let go of the ball, they stick their fingers in even further. Fists, and even boots, are fair game because we are playing a very physical contact sport, but gouging is a premeditated act of violence, nothing at all like a heat-of-the-moment punch thrown in anger or frustration. There's little referees can do about it. They can't see what goes on in the middle of rucks and mauls. We have to police it ourselves. If I see any of our players suffering in this way I have no second thoughts about taking the law into my own hands. If it means getting sent off or cited for my actions, so be it. I feel very strongly about this issue and I'm quite prepared to stand up and be counted, and bear the consequences. In the European Cup game at Pau in 1996 some bloke had his finger in the corner of Wellsy's eye up to the second knuckle. Despite all manner of skulduggery we won 19–16. Against Toulouse, down there in 1997, Eric Miller was done badly; Wig and I received a bit; and the guy who did Backy was yellow-carded. Once again, you see, we had them worried. The French only really resort to this sort of thing when they're in trouble: we won 22–17. Even the spectators were spitting at us. And then against Pau, in the quarter-final of that year's European Cup, Wig was again poked in the eye. I went absolutely ballistic, running round whacking people in revenge, and abusing the referee at every opportunity. After the game, Bob Dwyer and Duncan Hall, our coaches at the time, told me I shouldn't have reacted in that way, but my attitude is that if someone is doing that sort of disgusting thing to one of my team-mates I'd rather be sent off than do nothing about it. I hope if I ever get into a similar situation, or if I'm backed into a corner and in a pile of shit, the boys will come and help me out. You just can't be poking people in the eyes. It's not just confined to France, either. I've been on the receiving end over here during a couple of league matches at Bath and Bristol. And I reckon I know the identity of the culprits. You grab their fingers for future reference. Both are internationals. One a prop, the other a hooker. You put the names to them.

Kicking or punching someone from behind, 'blindsiding' them, when they can't see it coming, is also pretty cheap. We played Saracens down at Vicarage Road over Christmas during the 1997–98 season when the pair of us were vying for the top spot in the Premiership. Needless to say, it got very fraught. Something blew up, inevitably, and François Pienaar ran up behind Martin Corry and clobbered him on the side of the head from the blind side. All the boys went berserk – you can cause some serious damage doing that, broken jaws and what have you. Pienaar collected some fists for that. Everyone piled in. What's the ref going to do? Who's he going to send off? It's complete mayhem. The ref just gets confused, doesn't he? All he wants to do is calm things down and get the game going again. He'll talk to both captains and that's about all he can do in the circumstances.

Squeezing someone's balls is commonplace but it's hardly going to kill them. I remember playing Northampton in a cup semi-final a few years back. We were stuffing them up front when Matt Dawson – he was only a young lad then – got on the wrong side of a maul. I ran in and forearmed him right in the bollocks and he went down like a sack of spuds! He never got on the wrong side of the ball again – that did the trick, all right. Many's the time I've had my balls squeezed and, I can tell you, you do release the ball a bit quick when someone grabs your bollocks. It's self-preservation, really. You just have to protect your privates. To hell with the ball. It's a natural reaction, isn't it? Then there's biting and fish-hooking – sticking your fingers in the corner of someone's mouth and yanking away. I've also heard of fingers being shoved up people's backsides, but I've never come across it at close quarters. The last thing I want to be doing is sticking my fingers up some-one else's arse!

Violence can erupt at any time, often right from the kick-off – as in that infamous Wales–England game in Cardiff which subsequently got the likes of Dawe, Chilcott and Richard Hill, the skipper, into a load of trouble. You must have the personnel for the job, of course. And, yes, on occasions there will be opponents who are targeted in this way. You'll be told to get into these boys early because they're not going to be keen on mixing it. The opening five minutes will be hit, punch, stamp, cheap-shot anyone you can get hold of. You know they haven't got the bottle for physical confrontation. You know they will back away sooner or later because they haven't the balls for the job. So you pummel them until they do. The reverse side of this scenario is when you visit a place like Toulouse where you've got Califano, Soula and Tournaire waiting for you in the front row and you know full well they're going to be every bit as hard as you. You know if you don't go out there and match their ferocity from the outset, they will be doing exactly the same to you as you do to others. Then it can lead to two things: either a massive punch-up or a mutual respect develops where they know that if they cross that certain line they'll get it all shoved back at them. Above all else, though, you've got to have the players in the team with the right mentality, otherwise it's a waste of time. You can't tell players to cut up rough unless they have it in them.

By contrast, on occasions, trouble can simmer the entire game before finally exploding into violence. For instance, Leicester have always been renowned for possessing a strong scrummage, so the opposition will continually try to mess us around. The scrum is forever collapsing or being reset. If the ref can't control the opposition, *you* must. You inevitably take out your frustration by sticking one on somebody. Then, it might be one of our players has just been shoved off the ball, been whacked, given stitches or had to go off for treatment as a result of some foul deed the referee has missed. The next scrum, in those circumstances, is a vehicle for retribution. This kind of bother tends to kick off late in the game when you've got the result in your pocket. Your mind turns to other things. The guy opposite may be someone you dislike. You give him a dig for luck, to satisfy that primitive urge. Sounds a bit mindless, I know, but it goes on all the time.

In point of fact, during any game that has become tense and a little frantic, any excuse to get in there and cause some havoc is great and difficult to pass up. There was an instance of this against Northampton in 1998–99. Pat Howard killed a ball – and was quite rightly sin-binned for it – but Matt Dawson has come in and kicked him in the head. Had there not been a player holding me back while all this was going on I'd have punched the hell out of

Dawson because there's no excuse for what he did. In those situations you have to retaliate in defence of your team-mate. I received quite a few letters of complaint afterwards, saying that if I was going to go on to a rugby pitch in such an aggressive frame of mind perhaps I should find myself another sport. That struck me as strange. Put what happened into a non-rugby scenario. Your best mate is being attacked. What do you do? Stand back? Your brother, your sister, your mother and father have been punched before your very eyes. How would *you* react? I think most people would react in the same way as me. I most certainly would if it was my family, and I consider the guys I play alongside as close to family as it can get. I make no apologies for reacting the way I do. I'll do so every day of the week if necessary. I have no qualms about it, whatever criticism it may bring down on me. I can live with myself a lot more easily for doing something instead of letting it go because I'd not got the balls to take action.

Not that you can get away with murder nowadays. The cameras catch most things, don't they? If someone is caught on video, or by the ref, poking an opponent in the eye, they should be banned for a fair old time. I have no problem with that. Other punishments I'm less sure about. If you get done for stamping, I feel 60 days is a hell of a long stretch for something that goes on all the while. Although you don't want to encourage wanton use of the boot in the game – you want to attract kids into the sport and you need to have parents wanting their kids to play the game – it's boys being boys, really. It's merely blokes doing what kids do in the playground. And you must be consistent. Austin Healey got eight weeks for stamping on Kevin Putt in the London Irish game, but Kevin Yates did something similar to a guy at Wasps and received only four weeks. Rugby could learn a lot from football. If you are sent off there a certain number of times you receive a three-match ban. In other words, rugby needs set punishments for set offences. Tot up your points, your yellow cards or whatever, and impose a suspension after a certain total is reached. It's so hit-and-miss at present. Are you being punished for the crime or are you being punished for who you are? It's all very odd to me.

I feel strongly that the game should be allowed to be more physical, for example in the way we use our feet to remove opponents from contact situations. This might lead to some borderline incidents as regards what constitutes legal play and what constitutes violent play, but if we don't do something physically in this area players will continue to lie on the ball all day and you'll never get the ball back. Of course, the All Blacks would just run straight over the guy — but if you do that here you'd be off the pitch.

I think we have a problem in our game today in that young players, by the time they're 18, 19 or 20, have been so over-coached regarding their behaviour on the pitch that all the nastiness has been extracted from them. Someone like Bath's Andy Long, for example, is immensely talented, far more talented than I am, but the raw aggression so vital in the front-five forwards has been coached out of him. Selectors fight shy of aggressive players because they are harder to handle. I'm sure that's why I was not capped earlier — I was too hot to handle. Regardless of how badly behaved this type of player appears, coaches must utilise this aggression by channelling it and disciplining it. I've become far more disciplined over the years because I don't want to miss out or let my mates down.

Let's give our young players with aggression something to aim for. Give them an opportunity and I'm positive they'll take it. The way we programme our youngsters at the moment results in good players, yes. But they're all soft in the head. There are no hard boys around. I've not seen any coming through in the last eight years. That can't be good for our game.

SIX

BEST OF ENEMIES

HOOKER is very much a specialist position. It's also a highly confrontational position. You're one on one with your opposite number. This does lead to a degree of rivalry, the odd feud even. Some rivals you rate, some you don't, but if someone gets picked to play for England ahead of me on merit I'll hold my hands up. One thing's for sure, of all the hookers I've faced, the one I dreaded playing against the most was Graham Dawe.

When I broke through into the senior ranks, the premier hookers in England were Brian Moore, John Olver, Kevin Dunn and Dawesy. Mooro won all the caps but there's no doubt in my mind who was the toughest opponent. Graham Dawe is a hard, hard bloke; a Cornish farmer, small, strong and wiry. There's a story that says before one Leicester–Bath game, during the on-pitch warm-ups, I deliberately ran past Dawesy as he was doing some press-ups and trod on his fingers. Well, it's quite true. I did step on his hands. You don't get that close to Dawesy unless it's on purpose! He never said a thing. He hardly ever said anything when you played against him. If you did anything untoward, he'd just look you in the eye and grit his teeth. You knew then he'd be coming back at you firing on all cylinders. I learnt a few things from him. He'd always have his knee up when the scrum was about to engage, for example, so you ended up hitting it with your head. Also, if the two front rows were standing up facing each other, he'd be digging the studs on his heels into your toes. I'm sure I used to get on his nerves with my antics in my mischievous youth. Before one cup game against Bath, I did a television interview from a farm with a pot-bellied pig that I nicknamed Dawesy! I think he's forgiven me. In fact, he's a really good bloke off the pitch, very down to earth. I'm sure he respected opponents who gave him a dig back, especially as I was so much younger than him. What made Dawesy so outstanding in my book was his consistency. You never had an easy game against Graham Dawe.

Brian Moore was a different personality altogether. He's a very complex person. I played against him several times, yet he never spoke to me afterwards or had a beer with me. That's the way he was – very competitive. At club level I never rated Mooro as particularly good – I always outplayed him, in my opinion, whenever we took on Harlequins. Mooro in an England shirt was a different proposition. He was very good at international level and once he reached that stage, I think he tended to save himself for it. His principal attributes were his competitiveness, obviously; he was a first-class talker, always moaning and trying to influence the referee; he was skilful and gutsy. He was certainly not soft. I can recall a game between 'Quins and Bath at the Stoop in which Dawesy punched and kicked him all afternoon. Mooro just kept staring at Graham, saying: 'I'm still here, Dawesy, I'm still here!' That's the way he was. He was a hard person in that he could take it but he was never much at dishing it out.

My first main rival was a lad called Andy Fields when we were competing for the England Colts spot. I didn't make the final squad, so when the Midlands played England I spent the entire game beating him in any way I could: I kicked him, hit him, spat at him – anything would do. That's what junior rugby had taught me to do. Now, Andy Fields was not a bad bloke really, but he had been to Millfield public school and I definitely had a chip on my shoulder at that stage. It was the haves and have-nots, wasn't it? I had this preconception that if you didn't attend the right school or play with the right club, you didn't get selected. I thought all public schoolboys were tossers. Gradually I learnt there are some great people who go to public schools, that there are good guys and bad guys, as there are in any comprehensive. But, back then, because I went to a comprehensive and played for a poxy junior club – though to me it wasn't poxy – I thought the world was against me. I had a bit of an attitude problem. I was convinced the selectors didn't like my aggression or the way I conducted myself. As it turned out, that aggression stood me in good stead for what was to come. I did make the England Under-21 side, and by the time you get to that stage rugby has become more of a man's game and the physical elements are more and more prevalent. As for the social thing, I soon learnt that rugby is a great leveller. At the age of 20 I was playing against Brian Moore, the England hooker, a solicitor and a very wealthy man – and there was I, Richard Cockerill, a boy from the village, a boy from the comprehensive, an antiques restorer earning £28.50 a week. But once you were on the rugby pitch nothing else counted beyond your ability to play.

My principal rival at U21 level, and on most occasions since, I suppose, was Mark Regan. I get on with most of my rivals –

socially I get on pretty well with Phil Greening and Neil McCarthy, for instance – but I've never got on with Regan. I dislike him with a passion. I feel a little bitter, probably, because he enjoyed opportunities denied me, but in addition to that I just don't like him as a person – all his good ol' West Country boy business gets on my nerves. I've got no time for him whatsoever.

The other hooker on the international scene besides Norm Hewitt (more of him later) with whom my name is often linked – probably because we're similar sorts, really – is James Dalton of South Africa. Joel Stransky told me that Dalton was interviewed back in South Africa on the subject of the world's current crop of hookers. He replied that Fitzpatrick's a good player and so on, until the interviewer mentioned my name, saying: 'Richard Cockerill's got a bit of a reputation – what do you think of him?' All Dalton said was: 'Cockerill is a cockroach!' That's all he'd say about me. We got off to a bad start when England played South Africa at Twickenham in November 1997. He conceded a few penalties and I kept tapping him as I ran by, saying: 'Thanks, James!' Of course, he got his own back during the return Test down in Cape Town the following summer. We were under the cosh in this one, eventually losing 18–0, and he was calling us a bunch of losers. 'Cockerill, do you ever win a Test match?' Well, everyone knows he missed the 1995 World Cup final through suspension, so I responded by asking him to show us his winner's medal. He didn't like that at all!

The two top men of the southern hemisphere have to be Phil Kearns of Australia and the one and only Sean Fitzpatrick of New Zealand. I've twice played against Kearns, though he was probably past his prime. Unfortunately, I never got to play against Fitzpatrick, which is a great shame. He was almost certainly the greatest hooker of the modern era but he was injured during the 1997 tour over here. He would have been a nice yardstick to measure myself against. Bob Dwyer was once quoted as saying I possessed some of Fitzy's qualities, his abrasiveness and competitiveness, his talking and so on. I doubt if I could have ruffled Fitzy's feathers but I'd like to have had a go. He was so good at the technical aspects of his game, he got about the pitch, he understood the game; and he was a fantastic talker. It almost got to the stage when he reffed the game! Referees were in awe of him by the end, a situation which had to work in the All Blacks' favour. The strange thing is that when Fitzpatrick talked he was being competitive, but when I talk I'm nothing but a gobshite! It's the same distinction between me and Mooro.

I think I can say that I've never had any aggravation with hookers from the other home nations. Keith Wood is a good boy, and maybe he even outdoes me in the dressing-room from what I saw on the Lions video. Keith plays different rugby to me – he's a run-arounder – but, like me, he's very passionate about his game and never more so than when he represents his country. Of the Welsh hookers I've met, Garin Jenkins is more of a grafter, whereas Barry Williams is a good ball player, though not perhaps the best of scrummagers. Barry's the Keith Wood type; I'm more the Garin Jenkins.

I missed last season's French match through injury, so the first time I met Raphael Ibanez was when Leicester played the World XV after we'd won the Premiership this year. He's another good, hard player and a sound bloke. I've got a lot of time for him. We went out to dinner with our partners after the match. The French hooker I probably know better than any other is Mons Soula of Toulouse. The French say Soula is an older version of me. The red mist comes down occasionally, the eyes pop out and away he goes! We have knocked lumps out of each other these past few seasons in the European Cup. The philosophy of French front rows is that rugby is a game of pride, which is why they are so aggressive – they don't want to let themselves down and lose face. Soula has come up to me and said: 'You're a good player – you have a big heart.' To me, that's a fantastic compliment, the ultimate, in fact. Compliments from your fellow professionals are the greatest accolade. We're obviously never going to be bosom pals on the field, but after the games in Toulouse we always have a beer or two in his bar.

The French and the Argentinians are the most renowned scrummagers in the world, especially the latter, as I can vouch from personal experience over there in 1997. The French tend to squat, as if they were lifting weights in the gym, and try to get underneath you and then stand up. That's a very hard move to compete against because it's a lot tougher to hold something down than it is to push something up. On their own ball they stay down but on ours they stand up, so you can't push or get a wheel going. It makes the scrum a mess and they may get a penalty out of it.

The essence of all forward play these days is technique. You can have a really big, strong guy with poor technique and a small guy with good technique and the latter will always be the better player. Scrummaging today is more of a pushing context than a hooking contest, although I still challenge anyone who thinks it's easy to sit in the middle of those two big guys and hook the ball cleanly, to go and try it for themselves. There's a helluva lot of weight coming through you. It's not a matter of the ball being stuck in and me putting my foot up. Perhaps the hooker's role is not as skilful as it was ten or fifteen years ago, but it's certainly more physically demanding than it's ever been. Packs are getting bigger and more powerful all the time. A forward's strength, technique and mentality must be first class. You need to be athletic, much more than in the old days when props, in particular, tended to be big fat guys who merely trotted from scrum to lineout.

The scrummage is a science in itself. You must get there early, set and make ready to engage. As soon as the opposition look half-ready, you hit them as they come in, while they're still upright. That's the ideal scenario. The best technique revolves around your feet, back and shoulders. You cannot take all the weight just through your back or else you are going to end up in a lot of pain. You have to ensure you use your legs and your back together. This way the weight goes through your body into the ground. Your biggest muscles are in your legs – that's where you must take the weight – not your back. You keep your back and legs in line so that when the weight comes through your neck it goes straight down your body into your feet and into the ground. If you ever start getting your legs straight but your back bent right over, so you're at right angles, you're going to wind up with your head touching your knees – and that's not very comfortable!

I always bind over the shoulders of my props onto their armpits, not their shorts. I don't like my props to bind on my shorts, either: it's too restricting. I get them to bind higher up my body so my hips and legs are reasonably free to get across to the ball. I hardly ever attempt a strike against the head: because the back rows have to stay bound, we tend to work at getting the wheels on. For example, if you've got a scrum on the left touchline, you try to wheel them by the tight-head driving forward, which moves the ball further away from their fly-half while bringing your flanker closer to him. They will try to push their loose-head up to counter that, perhaps allowing their number 8 to pick up from the base and drive though.

The worst situation facing the front row comes at engagement. If you don't get it right you can hit the top of your head on the opposition's shoulders, and then you tend to be pushed down. It's not funny – you're getting four to five hundred kilos up through your backside and into your head! If the scrum collapses you end up on top of your head with the second rows still pushing – you're literally driven into the ground. I've had a few narrow squeaks where I thought serious injury was in the offing. Your chin gets tucked under and you're driven into a ball. That can be scary. Playing against a decent side is fine because they'll want to push, which makes for a good competition because that's just what you want to do as well. Weaker packs are the problem. If you're too strong for them, all they are interested in doing is collapsing the scrum because if they are on the ground they can't go backwards. And what's the referee going to do about it? He'll only give a penalty to one side or the other; and at international level that tends to be against the stronger pack as it evens things up.

The most awkward individual to scrummage against was Jeff Probyn, a view I'm sure would be echoed all over the world. We had some great tussles with him. He had such very narrow shoulders and you had problems seeing and hooking the ball because he took you so low. Sammy Southern, at Orrell, was another awkward bastard, as was their hooker Neil Hitchen. When I first joined Leicester, Orrell were a major force in English rugby and their front row was a tough proposition. They used to hit the scrum quite softly, making you think this was all pretty comfortable, but as you caught sight of the scrum-half coming down to address the ball to the scrum, Southern would turn his shoulder and lower it, easing the loose-head out as a result, and bringing all the weight of the tight-head and hooker right into your face. Half the time you couldn't even see the ball, let alone get into a position to hook it. Gary Pearce of Northampton was exactly the same: narrow shoulders, big head. Your loose-head ended up outside his shoulders because he was so narrow. If the hit wasn't dead right with those kind of guys I received all the weight through me instead of the loose-head absorbing most of it. These days things are a bit easier. Props are mostly squarer and they're less tricky to scrum against. Someone like Daz Garforth is an immense scrummager, for instance, but he'll never be as awkward a customer as Probyn, Southern or Pearce, because he's too big and too square to adopt those troublesome body positions. There are no props today in the Probyn mould. Coaches don't look for that kind of physique or shape any more. The nearest you'd get might be Paul Wallace, who's squat and can be effective if you fail to keep him square. Small props can get underneath their opponents, of course, but if the guy opposite is four to five stone heavier than him it's a helluva job to lift him. The likes of Os du Randt are 20 stone plus, and that's a lot of weight to be getting under. Having said that, this size factor does tend to be given too much importance. If a guy like Wallace can do the job he should be picked. It was said I was too light at 16 stone and yet I've played against the best packs in the world and held my own with no problem whatsoever. It's the Neil Back syndrome again. The press get it into their heads that size is the key to success up front. If they want big props, for example, let them name some. If there are any bigger props than Victor Ubogu, Phil Vickery, Daz Garforth, Graham Rowntree and Trevor Woodman, where are they? We don't produce 20-stone-plus props over here. And if you weigh that much, you've got to run around with it! Look at South Africa. They've selected the two biggest props they can find, yet they're probably playing their worst rugby of recent years.

Darren, Graham and I are very proud and protective of our reputation as a scrummaging front row to be feared. We've been together a fair time now. Our first game was at Sheffield on the opening day of the 1992–93 season. Wig (so called on account of either a dodgy schoolboy haircut or the size of his ears – earwig) had been in the club's Youth XV and was the longest established, making his first-team début in 1990; Daz arrived from Nuneaton the season before me. The Welford Road crowd soon warmed to our wholehearted approach because a banner appeared on the Crumbie Terrace praising the ABC Club, referring to the letters the front row wore on their shirts. We have to wear numbers these days but the famous letters are still carried on our shorts. I don't think it's arrogant to say that most front rows in the Premiership raise their game against the infamous ABC Club. We are no longer unknowns. We're the yardstick by which Premiership front rows are measured, and several clubs have narrowed the gap between them and us, for example, importing foreigners like Pagel and Mendez at Northampton, Grau at Saracens and Leota at Wasps. We've not yet appeared together for England in a full international, although we did combine against the Premiership Allstars in one of the World Cup warm-up matches. We have played *en bloc* for the Barbarians on a number of occasions, notably in the Tests against Ireland and Scotland. We are very close to each other, on and off the pitch. Graham and Darren were ushers at my wedding. I'm not sure whether Sarah-Jane thinks I'm married more to them than to her! My loyalties are split. I'd certainly do anything for them.

When all is said and done, however, the front row is only as good as the five behind it. If there is no contribution from the back five of the scrum, the front row will be largely ineffective. Hard, honest grafters, like we have at Leicester in Martin Johnson and Fritz van Heerden, are the sort you need immediately behind you. They may possess talents in other areas that make them extra special commodities, but the second row and the back row must have the desire to be a part of the scrummage. Some aren't too keen on scrummaging and would much rather just run around the park doing the fancy stuff. You must attend to the former, a fundamental requirement of forward play, before you go gallivanting about.

In the final analysis, successful forward play is 80 per cent attitude and desire against 20 per cent technique. It's frequently all in the mind.

SEVEN

ME AND NORM

I have a reputation for being a bit of a talker during a game, and it's well deserved. I like nothing more than to wind up opponents in an effort to distract them and put them off their game. When I've done it for Leicester the press tend to hammer me, saying I'm 'puerile' or 'as irritating as a rash'. But after I'd wound up Norm Hewitt by talking to him as he was leading the All Blacks in the Haka before the Old Trafford Test in 1997, I was suddenly elevated to something like hero status. You just can't win with the press. Nothing surprises me about journalists any more. Anyway, the press eventually enjoyed a field day with me and Norm Hewitt because, when England visited New Zealand the following summer, the two of us hit the headlines once again – this time over an 'alleged' brawl in the street. All in all, quite a story that needs putting straight.

To start at the beginning: I was surprised to be facing the All Blacks in that Old Trafford Test. I didn't see myself getting any more caps after the two in Argentina. England did have another international that summer of 1997, in Australia, for which Mark

Regan and Phil Greening were selected. Greening dropped out and I made the bench, which pleased me enormously because I'd rather be there than not at all, but I thought that was that. When the 1997–98 season began, the selectors seemed to be looking at all sorts of people. I was fifth choice behind Regan, Greening, Simon Mitchell of Wasps and Andy Long of Bath. I wasn't even invited to train with England. Clive Woodward was now the England coach in place of Jack Rowell, and John Mitchell, the All Black and coach at Sale, had been appointed as coach to the forwards. That weekend we were due to play Bath in the Premiership at Welford Road. Regan and I had got on all right out in Australia – I don't like him much but had made an effort to pass pleasantries and so on for the sake of team unity – but the Friday before this crunch game I picked up the *Leicester Mercury* to read Regan quoted as saying I was 'nothing special'. This gave me so much motivation I absolutely battered him next day and we thrashed Bath 33–22. We out-scrummaged them to such an extent that Regan was substituted. I derived a load of satisfaction from that.

The immediate result of that game was my being called into the squad. John Mitchell is a good fella. He sees talent and seeks ways to harness it. Apparently, he'd attended a selection meeting where my name came up and I'd been shouted down. He disagreed and said I should be introduced into the squad. So, all of a sudden I jumped from number five to number two, behind Andy Long, and was on the bench for the Australian Test at Twickenham. With two more Tests to follow against New Zealand and one against South Africa, it was a good position to be in. Both Andy Long and Will Green made their débuts in the front row against Australia, and, in all honesty, we struggled in the scrums in the first half. I managed to get on as a 'blood' replacement for a few minutes and steadied things up. At half-time Clive put me on. We drew the match 15–15 and I was picked to start the following week against the All Blacks at Old Trafford.

I've always been a bit of a Jack-the-lad and one who played to the crowd, and I'd told myself that if ever I got the chance I'd play this up to the hilt. People relate to my personality on the field as much as they do to my rugby ability. I had an opportunity to express myself and was going to seize it with both hands. I never thought I'd be picked again for England, so this was all a bonus to me. I thought that if I was going to be dropped eventually I might just as well do exactly what I wanted to do.

The build-up through the week was nerve-wracking. We watched New Zealand play our A team on the Wednesday night. It was a strong A side but their 'dirt-trackers' thrashed us. All the press said England would be beaten by 40 or 50 points on the Saturday. Come the day, and Old Trafford, the 'theatre of dreams', as they call it, is a fantastic arena in which to play. For me, this was the be all and end all of life at the time. It was only my fourth cap. All I wanted to do was prove I could go out there and get stuck in. All these famous names were lined up against us: Zinzan Brooke, Ollo Brown, Ian Jones – players I'd only seen on television. I couldn't believe I was actually going to play against them. I was unbelievably nervous. I was so scared and yet really pumped up at the same time. I could have fought the world, wanting to prove myself. John Mitchell had placed a lot of faith in me, as had Clive to a certain extent. I wanted to repay that faith and put up a good display for the thousands in the stands and the millions watching on television all over the world. I wanted to show I had the balls to do the job.

I had seen videos of the match when Ireland walked towards the challenge of the Haka and I thought how I'd love to do precisely the same. Even though what happened at Old Trafford wasn't premeditated, in some ways it couldn't have worked out any better. I didn't know who led the Haka, I just wanted to get into his face and say, 'Come on, then! Let's get it on!' We'd sung the national anthem, which is pretty emotional in itself. I'm a very patriotic person, a very proud Englishman. Many countries seem to take more pride in their country than we do. Not me. Some of our players don't sing the national anthem with the same gusto as me. Some prefer to stay quiet. Each to his own. I'm not embarrassed to belt out the national anthem. I've often been close to tears, thinking of my folks up in the stand. It's an emotional moment and I want to make the most of it. When you first play for your country the anthems are one of the most moving parts of the entire experience. It's a motivational aid, I think. I love England. I'd do anything for my country. If there was conscription and I had to go to war for England, I'd do so willingly. As much as I like travelling and seeing other countries, I'm always glad to come home. I've never visited anywhere I'd rather live. I even love the English weather!

Usually the All Blacks perform the Haka on the halfway line, and as they were preparing to do it, Josh Kronfeld, the flanker, put his scrum cap down on the line. I booted it away! Before the game, someone had said we should stand up against our opposite number — it just so happened that mine was leading the Haka. Johnno was on one side of me and Daz was on the other. I can remember Johnno saying: 'Just look at him! Straight in the face!' To me it was like a fight in the pub or in the playground. I was scared. It was a totally alien environment — a situation, a stadium, all new to me. Here were the mighty All Blacks. They were laying down their challenge and I accepted it. What were we supposed to do, stand there like choirboys? I hadn't a clue what Norm Hewitt was shouting, so I kept telling him he could scream and yell all day and I would take it. We ended up virtually nose to nose and things might have kicked off but, thankfully, I suppose, they didn't. Had I planned it, I don't think I could have done it any better. As the All Blacks ran away, Johnno said to me: 'Cockers, you've done it now, mate!' I wanted to demonstrate my readiness for the task ahead. I received a load of criticism from the All Blacks' management afterwards. John Hart, the coach, said I was a disgrace, but I was not being disrespectful to their culture, which was one of the charges. They want to get a psychological edge and we, *I*, wanted to show we would not be fazed by it.

The game itself was largely uneventful in terms of the All Blacks looking to exact any form of revenge for what I'd done. I did get a 'shoeing' from Hewitt. The All Blacks wear these long, 22-millimetre studs and I've still got the mark Hewitt left on my arm. He never said anything to me during the match. At the end of the game, which we lost 25–8, we just shook hands and swapped shirts at the final whistle. The fireworks came the following summer out in New Zealand.

We played the first Test at Dunedin, known to the locals as the 'House of Pain'. We went out for a pre-match pitch inspection and the crowd were ready for me. The whole terrace opposite began chanting 'Cockerill is a wanker!'. We fielded an under-strength side, Danny Grewcock was sent off early for stamping, and we were well beaten 64–22. I did score a try and celebrated by hoofing the ball into the terrace. Hewitt had been on the bench, Anton Oliver being preferred in his place.

Later that night – or early the next morning, it's difficult to remember which – John Mitchell, Graham Rowntree and I go into town for a beer. We enter this bar, it must be two or three in the morning by now, and find Hewitt in there, badly pissed-up. He starts slagging English rugby, saying how shitty we are. I ask him how his arse feels with all those splinters in it from sitting on the bench. Then I really get to work on him. I start doing the Haka in front of him, slapping my thighs and sticking my tongue out. He seems to take it all right, considering he's got a reputation for being as much of a handful as I am. It's agreed we'll all move on somewhere else and we call a cab. It's one of those minibus-taxis as there's a few of us now. Hewitt gets in first, ahead of me, and as soon as I stick my head through the door to follow, he leathers me. Suddenly it all kicks off in the van, him and me going at it for all we're worth. My eye swells up straightaway and is a right mess. He's had a good, cheap shot at me but it's far from over. When we reach our destination I'm the first out of the taxi, and I'm waiting for him this time. When he gets out I smack him one and we end up brawling again – right down the street. He's in jeans and a rugby shirt but I'm dressed in my posh England gear, so that takes a pasting, doesn't it?

The following morning the word had got round, and when I come down to breakfast sporting a huge black eye, there are dozens of journalists blocking the doors. Apparently, the two students who'd been following us around and were in the taxi with us had sold the story to the newspapers. Clive's father had just died and he was preparing to go home. Obviously, he wasn't in the best of moods. I told him I'd had a spot of bother – but no one knew about it. Then he arrived back in London to see the story spread all over the back page of the *Daily Mail*! Later that morning

I got a call from Hewitt, saying how he was afraid this incident would get him booted out of the All Blacks. So we tried to get it all toned down to the level of a play-fight.

The following Tuesday we played the New Zealand Maoris at Rotorua. Greening started the game but when the announcement was made that he was coming off and I was going on, the crowd went mad. As it happened, he stayed on. It was a hair-raising moment all the same. In the second Test, Oliver went off injured and Hewitt came on to a tremendous cheer. Before there was a chance of anything kicking off between us, he snapped the cruciate ligament in his knee. I went in to have a chat with him afterwards and he was sound, no hard feelings. I think he appreciated that we'd got him out of a scrape and preserved his All Black career.

You definitely can play mind games with opponents, or some of them at least. You can tell which players are nervous and therefore susceptible to some banter. They've made mistakes, perhaps, and you hammer it home. If I'm playing against Regan, his throwing-in is not the greatest, so as soon as he begins making a few errors I start on him because I know throwing-in is something he's worried about and he's trying extra hard to concentrate on it. I'll attempt to break that concentration and undermine his confidence with comments like: 'Where's lightning going to strike next?' or 'There's another Scud – where's it gonna land?' The actual content of what I say is meaningless, it amounts to nothing. 'Your wife's ugly . . .' It's the constant stream of abuse that matters. My opponent eventually gets so pissed off he becomes more concerned with what I'm saying and doing than concentrating on what he should be doing. If Regan throws a bad ball it might be: 'Oh, is it our scrum?'; if you're playing someone in the relegation zone it could be: 'Going down?' or 'Got a job for next season, have you?' It doesn't matter how mindless the comments are. Anything that comes into your head will do. The object is to get in their face and stay there until your words take effect. Kicking the ball away when someone's trying to pick it up for a lineout; getting the ball when it's their throw and trying to throw it in yourself – anything like that will do.

In some respects it's more a form of self-motivation than attempting to put the opposition off their game. If you're laying down a challenge in this way, you're half-expecting them to respond, and you can't offer someone a fight if you're not psyched up for it yourself. You'll bump into them, trip them up as they walk past. You're nicely on the edge, waiting for them to retaliate – which is where you want to be.

Talking doesn't get to me. If I'm ever on the receiving end of some banter or abuse I say: 'Listen, mate. *I* do the talking! Don't copy me, do your own thing. I'm the boy that does this!' Originally, when people began commenting on my talking, I couldn't understand it or appreciate why they were so interested in it because it was what I'd done ever since I was a kid. It just goes to show how few characters there are in the game. If people think it's such a big deal – love it or hate it – it just emphasises how boring rugby players must be nowadays. Some try to be like me, but they can't – there's only one of me! Some say I'm like Brian Moore, but I'm not. We might share similar attitudes but he was totally different to me in the way he conducted himself. I want people to remember Richard Cockerill for what I am. You should be what you are, not something you're not.

EIGHT

LIVING WITH CELEBRITY

THE Haka incident put me on the map. I don't know why people make a fuss of how I go about things. It just goes to show how dull rugby is becoming, with fewer and fewer 'personalities' in the game. My motto is anything for a decent wedge, so the opportunity to make a few quid on the after-dinner circuit or, better still, on television is fine by me. *OK* magazine even coughed up £1,500 to do a five-page spread on our wedding!

I've done all sorts of television in the last couple of years: *Live and Dangerous* on Channel 5, *Under the Moon* on Channel 4, *Not Melinda's Big Night In* with Gail Porter, *Late Tackle* for Central a couple of times. Probably the most memorable of these live appearances were those on *The Big Breakfast* and *On Side*. I didn't get to be 'on the bed' with Paula Yates but I did get to work alongside Denise Van Outen – or should I say Zig and Zag! These two glove puppets were dressed up in mini New Zealand shirts and took the piss out of me by doing their version of the Haka. They also had a male model in the studio, and Denise Van Outen and Johnny Vaughan tried to get me to agree to a 'makeover'. I was having none of that! The *On Side* appearance came after we'd beaten South Africa 13–7 at Twickenham in December 1998. We arrived back at the Petersham Hotel and John Inverdale, who presents the programme and is a very keen rugby man, was waiting for me. He'd been at the game and just asked me to be on Monday's show. It's quite a high-profile programme, so I was more than happy to oblige. He also had Stuart Pearce — known to football fans as 'Psycho' — as a guest, which was meant to fit in with my antics during the Haka, one of the subjects we talked about. The third guest was the champion Canadian sprinter Donovan Bailey. It was a great experience — and I got paid!

Obviously, I am acutely aware of my public image nowadays. I am always very conscious of the need not to make a spectacle of myself. When I was a young man — 17 or 18 — and first discovered ale, pubs and girlfriends, I would play rugby, drink as much beer as I could get into me, go into town and behave exactly as I wanted: push to the front of queues — 'What are you gonna do about it?' — and generally act in an obnoxious way because I didn't know any better. People who go out and deliberately try to cause trouble, like I did, are probably only trying to prove something: I'm macho, I'm hard, I'm a man. But I don't need to prove that any more. In the last two or three years I've gone on to the rugby field and played against the biggest, hardest, roughest rugby players in the world and I'm as good, as strong and as hard as they are. I get kicked. I get punched. It's a very physical sport. That's how I prove my manhood — on the rugby pitch.

When I go to the pub and have a few beers — not that there are many occasions when I can do so these days — I'm not looking for any bother. I get that every Saturday afternoon. People know who

I am. Some might think, 'He's a bit of a loony on the pitch, steer clear of him'; they think I'm some kind of lunatic because I've had my moments on the field now and again. No one has ever tried it on, and I never give anyone a reason to become involved. I'm always polite. If I bump into a guy, whether he's tiny or massive, I'll say, 'Sorry, mate,' because there's no need for aggravation. Someone might cut me up in the car, and most people would give them abuse, but I don't. That person cutting you up may be the club member who sits in the second row of the stand. It's the same if someone slips in front of you at the supermarket checkout. You drop your guard just the once and that's all it takes.

People come up and talk to me all the time. Often I can do without it. I've had enough of talking about rugby. But I've never abused anyone who tries to talk to me. I'll always say, 'Nice to see you, look after yourself.' I'll never consciously give anyone an excuse to think I'm a big-head or a prima donna, because I'm not. Some might look at me and think, 'Hooligan.' I'm short and stocky, I've got no hair, so I must be a thug, a dullard, someone not very bright or very nice. People try to label me but I'm just a working-class bloke, one of Maggie Thatcher's YTS kids. I think I can relate to the guys in the street who go to work all week and come to stand on the terraces every Saturday afternoon. I don't think I'm any different to the working-class guy who sweats in the factory and spends his money on a Saturday by coming to watch me play rugby. I can see how some higher-profile players might get themselves into trouble because, eventually, you do get pissed off with people wanting a piece of you, and may be tempted to say, 'No! Go away!' in a less-than-polite manner. I've not reached that stage yet, but I've come pretty close at times, especially straight after games when I'm knackered and I just want to get away to see my wife or my mum and dad. There can be two hundred people waiting for autographs you must sign, and, even though it can get very wearing, you have to remind yourself how lucky you are to be in this situation.

Players in the public eye do have a responsibility. It comes with the territory. To say you don't have a responsibility is a bit arrogant. On the other hand, everyone is human. The problem is that when you're in the public eye, you make one mistake, upset one person – even if you've been pleasant to a thousand others – and he tells his mate you're a wanker. And so it goes on. I was off, injured or on the bench, for one game at Welford Road and the dugout is very close to the crowd. Throughout the game I was effing and blinding at the ref. On the Monday I was called in by Peter Wheeler, Leicester's chief executive, to explain myself because a woman had written in complaining about my language.

I might be in a shop, buying a Mars Bar, for example, and someone will come up to me and say, 'Should you be eating that?' It can become very irritating. But the public think they own you, or a piece of you. They occasionally forget we're just ordinary guys who've worked hard to get where we are. I'm just a working-class lad from a small village who happened to become good at rugby. Otherwise I'm the same as everybody else. Some see me with a flash car and a nice house and they resent the fact that it all comes from sport. They don't necessarily recognise the sacrifices I've made. Nevertheless, I can't complain. The only time you can relax is at home or in the changing-room with the boys. Then you can be as crude and rude as you like, the same as all those lads who behave like that down the pub on a Saturday night. Professional rugby players can't do that any more.

The Welford Road fans do appear to have taken me to their hearts. You only earn that level of respect through your playing ability. The fans sense that I always give 100 per cent. Perhaps I am a showboater and a poseur sometimes, but you must also deliver on the pitch, do all the nitty-gritty first. I can respect players like Johnno or Daz who don't wish to get involved with that sort of thing and they respect my wish to do the opposite and develop a rapport with the crowd. There are so few characters in the game today who can do that. Perhaps when I've finished playing and maybe there are no characters left in rugby, people will start saying it's a shame someone like Richard Cockerill is no longer around. Everyone remembers the McEnroes and the Gascoignes more than the faceless ones, don't they?

I'm sure people become fans of a particular sport because they are frustrated performers at that sport. They'd love to play and behave the way I do. They come to watch a game of rugby, yes, but they want to be entertained – and I want to entertain them in return. Showboating now and then is my way of achieving that objective. I may have looked a complete and utter prat, for example, when I gave the Members' Stand a hugely extravagant theatrical bow after they'd applauded me for doing something uncharacteristically skilful in open play – a kick ahead and chase – during last season's West Hartlepool match, but if you can't laugh at yourself, who cares? They loved it and I enjoyed doing it. If it puts a smile on a few thousand faces, I'm more than content. I'll always wave, stick my thumb up or whatever to acknowledge any funny comment from a wag in the crowd. If you got no reaction from the crowd you wouldn't do it, would you? It's a relationship you have with them. If you're an unpopular player you wouldn't risk doing it, would you? I've just got this rapport with our fans and I am grateful for it. Let's face it, we don't want a bunch of faceless robots playing the game, do we?

I'll do anything for our supporters, as and when required. I make time for them. I don't think I've ever shunned a supporter by not signing an autograph or posing for a photograph. To me, the fans are the people who make Leicester tick. After the West Hartlepool game, when we were presented with the Premiership trophy, I must have been out on the pitch for an hour and a half, signing autographs, eventually standing there on my own while the rest of the lads were back in the changing-room getting showered and dressed.

One of my usual haunts is the children's hospital. I usually do these visits because I can relate to kids quite easily, still being a big kid myself. Some of these visits are great, kids with measles or whatever. But then I'll go in to see some child with cancer or another terminal illness. What do you say to them? 'Hi! How ya doin'? All right?' when they've perhaps only got weeks to live. How the hell can you imagine what they're feeling? You take in some kit or signed T-shirts for them in order to break the ice – then two weeks later you get a letter to say little Johnny, who you visited a fortnight ago, died last night. It's terrible. Leaves me gutted. Making this kind of visit, or donating kit to auctions, is a small sacrifice for me to make. Some of these kids see me as a kind of role model and others have little idea of who I am. It doesn't matter. I'm in a very fortunate position, being well paid for something I love doing. I owe it to myself to go out and do something for others. Hopefully, it means something to them.

Doing things like that often comes naturally, and I do feel a certain responsibility to put something back into the game which has given me everything I have. Another young lad wrote to me from Salisbury Juniors to say that his team were playing a game on the Saturday morning before coming to Twickenham for the Leicester v. Barbarians game – the annual match between the Premiership winners and a World Select XV. He was from Leicester but his dad was serving with the army down there. I rang up and told his father the lad could come into the changing-rooms and meet the players. After the game there was no sign of him, or so I thought. I was looking for this one lad. Then a steward tells me there's all 18 of the Salisbury side waiting for me! Most of the players had left for the bar, so I took them upstairs to meet the lot, Tigers and Baa-baas. It was no sweat for me. It's just nice to think you're making a difference for somebody's life. That's the way I look at it.

I've never abandoned my roots and keep in touch, for instance, with all the old Newbold rugby crowd. One of my England shirts is in the Barley Mow pub. Before we played Australia – out there – in 1998 I spoke to my mate Richard Cook and he said all the boys were going to watch the game in the Barley Mow in the early hours, have a few beers and then a bit of breakfast. I said that if Mick Smith, the landlord, opened up the pub for them, he could have my shirt. So there it is. Before we played France this year someone bet Cooky that I wouldn't be prepared to shout 'Come on the Barley Mow!' as I ran out on to the pitch. I obliged and the whole pub went wild. It was a perfect case of not forgetting my roots. I'm no different with the boys in Newbold to when I played with them. We treat each other just the same as always. I love it when I turn on my mobile phone the day after an international. There's usually 20 or so abusive messages on it from the Newbold lads who've gone down the Barley Mow, watched the match on telly and got legless!

Basically, you have to live two lives: your rugby life and your private life. If you allow your rugby life to enter your private life, it takes over. It's difficult to stop it from doing so. You need to be highly disciplined about it. It's very easy to fall into the trap of becoming highly pretentious. We stay in five-star hotels all the time, for example, and it can be easy to come home expecting the same treatment – which is not on, is it? Celebrity and domesticity have to be kept separate at all costs.

Rugby is my way of escaping from real life!

NINE

MY FRIENDS THE PRESS

JOURNALISTS write a load of bullshit. They do my head in the way they write things about people and the way they slag them off. I don't mind being criticised if I've played badly and the criticism is of my technique. But character assassination is different. I've been called a pantomime villain, a cartoon character made flesh, and been described as puerile, spiteful, tiresome and irritating. I still speak to the press because if I don't give them an opinion or response they'll make one up anyway. There aren't many journalists I like, that's for sure. Chris Goddard, on the *Leicester Mercury*, is a good guy. He's a truthful and honest reporter, not overly biased towards Leicester. Admittedly, he has to deal with us all on pretty much a daily basis, which may influence his writing, but he's not averse to criticising us when the occasion demands it, and he does so fairly by concentrating on the game rather than attacking personalities. Barrie Fairall of *The Independent* and now the *Telegraph* is a good fella who writes about the game rather than the personalities; Peter Jackson of the *Daily Mail* is a bit 'tabloid' in his approach, always looking for an angle, but he's not particularly personal in his criticism; Stephen Jones, in the *Sunday Times* – well, he's a Celt, isn't he, so he's never going to be too kind to the English! Most of the others are so full of shit.

I've never been two-faced in my life. If I think someone's an idiot, I'll tell them so. I'm honest and up front, and I just wish more people, especially the press, would be like that towards me. There are too many cowards who shelter behind words in newspapers or hide behind selection committees, refusing to tell you the truth. If someone asks me a question, they get a truthful answer. I don't care what people think about me as a result. I'll do what I do. I made a conscious decision to live my life that way at an early age. I wasn't going to conform to all the bullshit politics that runs through the press and selection procedures.

Take Paul Ackford, for example. As a former England international and British Lion he knows more about the game than most of the press – most of whom have never played the game to any degree – and when he started out with the *Telegraph* he confined himself to writing about the match he'd seen and was quite good. Now, he wants to be controversial via his column. After we'd battered Bath at Welford Road in 1997, he said I was a disgrace and asked if this kind of behaviour was what rugby was coming to. I felt compelled to write a letter to the *Telegraph* suggesting he was viewing the game through a pair of rose-tinted spectacles, looking back to a so-called golden age of rugby that never really existed. That weekend England played New Zealand at Old Trafford, the game in which I faced up to the All Blacks' Haka. After the match Ackford came up to me, shook my hand and said: 'Brilliant!' One week I was a bovver boy, the next I was a British bulldog.

After Ackford slagged me off on another occasion, he rang and left a message on my answerphone. I ignored it. Then he got me on my mobile. I said: 'What are you ringing me for? You don't like me' – that's how he'd started this article. He replied: 'I think we've got off on the wrong foot.' So I just said: 'No, you wrote that I was a disgrace.' I know journalists have a job to do but they can't write one thing one week and then expect us to be best mates the next. Ackford then wrote a good piece about me. Of course, when the press compliment you, you do love it: when they write bad things about you, it's shit! You must take the rough with the smooth because it's never going to go in your favour all the time.

Stuart Barnes is another former international who is poison, in the *Telegraph* or on Sky – not that you'd expect a Bath man to have anything good to say about someone from Leicester. He started saying I wasn't a good enough athlete to keep up with the speed of England's all-singing, all-dancing game, and that my throwing-in had gone to pot – as if hitting the jumper is all down to the thrower, which anybody with any sense appreciates it is not. He was angling to get Phil Greening into the side for the World Cup. He's entitled to his opinion. But he was a very average fly-half who never really made it in an international shirt – he could never get past Rob Andrew – and he's pretty bitter and twisted about it. He was nothing more than a good club player and a very average international player. England didn't do too well when he played. I think you'll find he played in ten Tests for England and they won only three of them – against Scotland, Fiji and Romania, so some general he was at fly-half. Criticism is fine but there is a line between criticism and personal abuse and he crosses it. I've got no time for Barnes in any shape or form. I don't respect him.

Despite this enmity with certain members of the press, I've never been driven to an eyeball-to-eyeball confrontation. There's no point, because they are always going to win. It's the power of the pen, isn't it? There have been occasions when I've been tempted, though. Eddie Butler wrote some stuff about me in an England programme. He accused me of being antagonistic and said that hopefully after the game someone would take me round the back of the stand and take me on one to one instead of me having a 70,000 crowd on my side. So, one day, perhaps, I'd like to take *him* behind the stand and we'll settle that one. And he was one of the softest players of the lot, allegedly, when he played for Wales! Once again there was nothing said about my playing ability – it was just character assassination, having a pop for no reason. I've got no time for that.

I accept that people like Ackford, Barnes and Butler have columns to fill and contracts to fulfil, but to achieve that end to the detriment of someone else is not on. A small, insignificant, throwaway comment about a player may damage that guy quite considerably, but they don't think about that, do they? These throwaway remarks, which mean nothing to them, are read by coaches, other players, and the family of whoever is being targeted. They start to sow seeds of doubt. Some people will base their opinion of those players on what they read in the newspapers or hear on the television. The attitude of the press towards a player can help form his reputation, be it good or bad. The public can't help reacting in that way.

What happens to a lot of players is that they come on to the scene at 21 or so and play well enough through their first season in the big time. No one knows who they are or anything about them, and they receive a load of rave reviews – then the following season everyone wants to knock them off their perch. The press start to get into them, they don't perform so well and they start

This is probably most people's mental image of me on a rugby pitch
© Neville Chadwick Photography

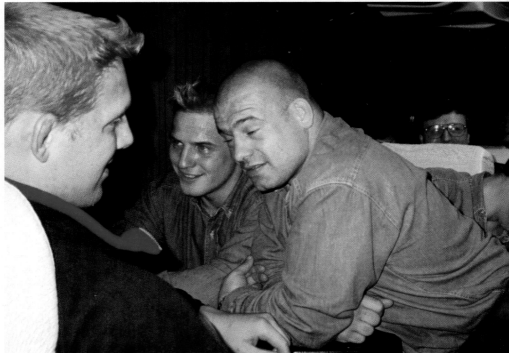

TOP: Daz, me and Wig in Baa-baas colours, and perfectly sober, I might add
ABOVE: There's never a dull moment on our team bus, even if Lewis Moody and Paul Gustar
are trying to ignore their bleary-eyed tormentor © Michael Tanner

ABOVE: Jumping for joy: we've just beaten Bath to secure the 1994–95 League title

ABOVE: Brian Campsell has his hands full trying to stop me exacting revenge on Wasps' Buster White, who has just stamped on Graham Rowntree © Andrew Maw

LEFT: Receiving a ticking-off from Señor Sklar, a visitor from Argentina, much to Mooro's obvious amusement © Andrew Maw

RIGHT: Playing for England A could get frustrating © Sportsline Photographic

TOP: My prized first England jersey, won out in Argentina © Michael Tanner
ABOVE: Training with the Royal Marines on Dartmoor before the 1999 World Cup: Yellow team (rear) Matt Dawson, Jason Leonard, Danny Grewcock, David Rees and Matt Perry, flanked by two instructors; (front) Neil Back and me with Coops, our IC

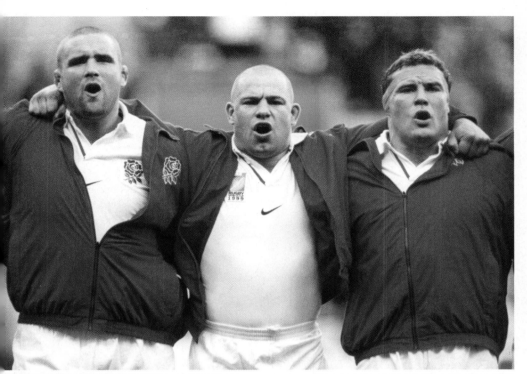

TOP AND ABOVE:
What wearing the red rose means to me © Fotosport

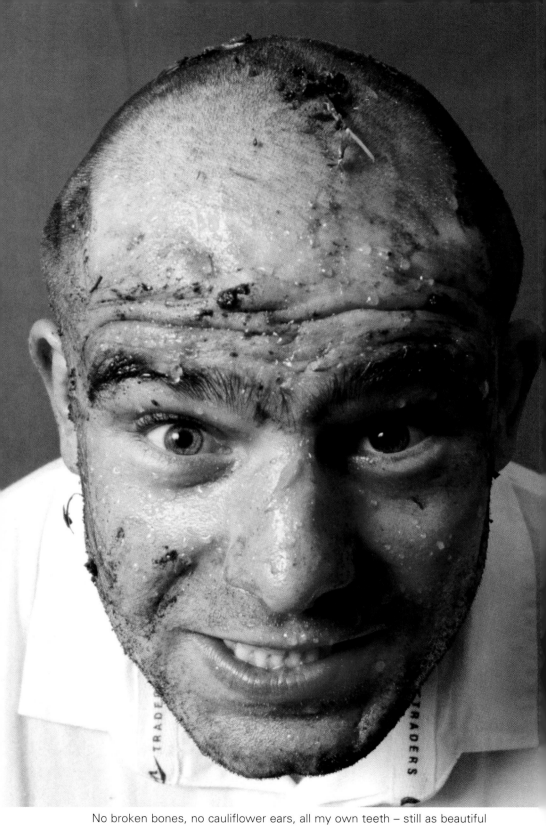

No broken bones, no cauliflower ears, all my own teeth – still as beautiful
as the day I was born! © Marc Aspland/*The Times*

getting disillusioned. Suddenly it's no longer a great world to be in. People are criticising you. Some players find this difficult to handle.

A prime example of this kind of sniping affecting a player is Graham Rowntree. Wig is a good, honest rugby player who'd do nobody any harm. He wouldn't even say a bad word about anybody. So when the likes of Ackford and Barnes write things such as he is a spent force, his England days are over, the Lions tour ruined him, Graham reads this in the paper and finds it hard to deal with. His family read this shit, and that upsets him further. To me, it's generally water off a duck's back, but I don't think the press realise how much these comments can hurt – the character slurs, 'he's lost the desire', or whatever. People who know me know the truth about my character. What *does* bother me is that people reading this shit who don't know me may think it's true. Rugby is only a game and what I do in public is only for that game. I couldn't behave like that in real life. Society wouldn't let me. People do tend to lose sight of that fact.

The English press always pick up on the negative. When the All Blacks win, the New Zealand press play it up, however well the side performed, whereas our press will say something like 'England didn't play well, they should have won by more points, they should have done this or that . . .' Foreign journalists do criticise – of course they do – but they always seem to emphasise the positive side of a game more than our guys do.

I suppose it's easier to criticise than to be positive, isn't it?

TEN

POSITIONS OF RESPECT

E VERYONE has to earn respect. Just because you are in a position of power or authority on the pitch, like a captain, coach or referee, doesn't mean you're better than everyone else. Because I'm an international doesn't automatically guarantee me respect from all the other players, for instance. If someone has been there and done it in rugby terms, he tends to get my respect. I respect Deano, not because he's the greatest manager of a rugby team in the world, but because he has played a lot of rugby, seen it and done it. It's the same thing with having Johnno as captain; enough said. And as far as referees are concerned, it's much easier to respect those who treat you respectfully, rather than in a schoolmasterly fashion – you and them, as it were.

The best referees are definitely those who talk to you and treat you as equals, people like Ed Morrison, Brian Campsell and Chris White. On the other hand, some, like Steve Lander – who's quite a good referee technically – treat you in a teacher-pupil sort of way ('I'm in charge, don't talk to me!') which tends to wind players up. Communication skills and man management are vital areas for good refereeing. Southern-hemisphere referees are much better, I think. We're very strict, very letter-of-the-law, whereas they referee more to the spirit of the game. Even off the pitch they're good blokes, which is a head start – not that you make a point of deliberately trying to fraternise with referees! But there's more to life than a game of rugby, isn't there? I can remember picking up Steve Lander after Backy knocked him over at the end of the 1996 Cup final when he'd given Bath the penalty try that won the game for them. Afterwards, up in the bar, he came across with his wife and kids and said: 'Thanks for that. It was getting out of hand. I was going to go after him.' I'd saved him from making a grave mistake and he was big enough to acknowledge the fact.

The main area for professional referees to work on is in the development of a rapport with players. Nobody likes being spoken 'at', do they? If there's a big problem we should be allowed to talk to each other. If I blow a gasket at some decision, Ed Morrison will say, 'Get on with it!', but the Steve Landers of the refereeing world will march you back ten metres. It's knowing how to handle people, isn't it? Don't get me wrong – our refs are good, they know the laws. One of our other problems stems from the fact that a referee is constantly being assessed. As a result, too many of them try to be the star of the show and ruin the game for players and spectators alike. They might be crossing the 't's and dotting the 'i's to impress the assessor sitting up in the stand, but that approach is not necessarily the best thing for the game. For the final Premiership match of 1998–99 against West Hartlepool, we had quite an inexperienced guy, a Mr Goodliffe, who was being assessed by Colin High, one of the top men in the country. This ref was a nightmare! He seemed to be there for his own game, to try and impress, to get good marks in order to further his refereeing career. John Wells spoke to Colin High about him and High said that on his most recent assessment he'd not been sufficiently strict. So this time he blew everything and destroyed the game as a result. The best referee is always the referee you don't even remember being in charge.

You see, a good game from the players' point of view is different to a good game from a referee's point of view. I'm sure it's frequently very difficult to referee games where people like me and Johnno, for example, are constantly debating every decision. But referees often don't help themselves. During a cup game with Richmond in 1998–99, Steve Lander sin-binned Johnno for stepping over a ruck and kicking the ball out of their scrum-half's hands. The ref wasn't even looking at the incident but all the Richmond players moaned. At the time, Lander said Johnno was hitting the ball down with his hand, but in his report he said Johnno had kicked the ball out of Pichot's hands. In the end, the white card was wiped off Johnno's record. Basically, Steve Lander was covering his back in that situation. He's a full-time referee who's getting paid good money, yet he said one thing on the pitch – picked up on his microphone by television – and in his report he wrote something else. Apparently, at the disciplinary hearing itself, he said he thought it was illegal to kick the ball out of someone's hands – which it isn't! So he didn't even know the specific law on that situation. Having said that, all the refs I've spoken to about the incident thought it was illegal as well. It's that schoolmaster mentality again: I'm in charge, I'm always right, I'll cover my arse to suit. When you're an amateur it's okay to make a mistake because you're not being paid, but when you're a professional and, like the players, getting paid for your performance, you must hold your hands up to a mistake. You cannot say one thing and then another.

Consistency is the other refereeing problem. Refs might be consistent in their decisions through one particular game but each referee is different from game to game. The ruck is a prime example. Can you dive in? Can you play the ball with your hands on the ground? Can you bridge over the ball? Some referees will let things go if the ball is coming out, for example. They say that's fine. In the southern hemisphere, if the ball is on your side and coming back, the refs don't care if you dive in, use your hands or whatever. If you've won it and it's coming back they don't care what happens. The ball emerges, the crowd sees more rugby, the players are happy, everybody's happy. Another instance of differing interpretation is that if the ball is at the number 8's feet and the scrum collapses, the southern-hemisphere referee will allow the scrum-half to get the ball away. If there's going to be an injury from the scrum collapse, it will already have happened; and by ordering another scrum, all you're doing is doubling the possibility of trouble, aren't you? The game is stopped; the crowd's getting bored. All the referee is doing if he blows up is exerting his authority. It's a waste of time. It's daft!

Nor am I happy with the tackle law. The attacking team gets looked after by the referee more than the defending side. If you are in there attempting to get the ball after the tackle, you must be on your feet – and half the time, even if you are on your feet, you get penalised. The outcome of this is that you commit as few people as possible to the ruck and spread the rest across the field in defence. If you commit all eight forwards to the ruck in order to try to win the ball, you've eight men out of the game; one to make the tackle and two more to help is enough. In the old days, the Dean Richards and John Wells era, you'd all get there and try to slow it down at the ruck. Not any more. But by having a defence spread across the pitch you take space away from the attackers once they've released the ball – which is perhaps not in the interest of spectators. The best form of defence at the tackle is exemplified by Backy, who is so short and strong. He stays on his feet, gets over and gets his hands on the ball. If he does that, and the guy continues to hold on to the ball, we win the penalty. In the final analysis, though, unless the opponent has bad technique, you are very unlikely ever to turn the ball over – which, of course, removes a significant confrontational situation from the game.

People talk about captaincy as if it involves some kind of mystical motivation and as if the captain must be a messianic leader of men. I don't think it's as complicated as that. In fact, I think it's reasonably simple. Leicester, for example, could almost play *without* a captain. The amount of quality players and the number of personalities within the team makes a captain unnecessary. Martin Johnson does a good job, but I don't know how good he'd be if he was captain of a bad team. He's never had to deal with that scenario and, hopefully, he never will. Too much is made of captaincy in my opinion. Johnno received all these accolades with the British Lions and then led Leicester to the Premiership title. But he led because he played! We'd miss him if he wasn't on the pitch because he's a world-class player, but we didn't win the Premiership because he was a good captain. We won because Johnno was a good player along with the other 25 who contributed throughout the season. Johnno's captaincy was not a deciding factor at all in us being successful. He's a fantastic figurehead, yes, and he's the best player – and the best players tend to be appointed captains in nine cases out of ten. England omitted Jerry Guscott because Phil de Glanville was appointed captain but, with all due respect to Phil, they shouldn't have done that. You should always pick the best players first, and then appoint your captain. Phil is no Jerry Guscott! The most important thing is that the players must respect the captain, not necessarily as a bloke but as a player. He must command his spot in the team.

There is no getting away from the fact that Johnno is a great leader. Basically, he's just one of the boys. He does nothing differently to the rest of us. He's earned respect by playing games and doing the job, talking sense instead of mouthing hollow words or a load of bullshit. It's deeds that count, not words. Johnno turns up for training on time. He rarely, if ever, misses a session. He works hard, does all the shitty work, works with the young lads, the old lads – anybody. He's not a prima donna. He works for the other guys. That's how people, captains especially, get the respect of their peers. A lot of the senior guys at Leicester are in the Johnno mould. If people don't train, for example, they get loads of stick for it, so they end up feeling bad about it. We also say to any new boys who try giving it a lot of banter, 'Get some games in', because that's how respect is earned. It's easy to play one season at Leicester and do well, but can you do it the next year, and the year after, and the year after that? Do it year in and year out and you're guaranteed respect.

Being captain of Leicester is probably a lot easier than being captain of Newbold. If you're captain of the Newbold first XV, as my brother was, you're forever ringing up players, organising the transport, the whole lot, in addition to doing the playing side of the job. Obviously, Johnno functions as a go-between for management and players, but his role is a lot simpler, and therefore easier, to be honest. Certainly, when push comes to shove, you want to follow Johnno into battle because he does everything he can for the players, he wants to play every game – even the unimportant ones – and when he says something you know he means it and there's substance to it. Dean and John Wells were likewise always pretty quiet in the dressing-room. There are generally several leaders in a team of whom some, like me, are the vocal ones, and they are allowed to get on with it. My relationship with Johnno is different to the one I had with Dean or Wellsy. I've come up through the ranks with Johnno and I tend not to take as much notice of him as I could because he's more of a buddy than an authority figure. There are times when I disagree with him but he's the skipper so I go along with his decision.

I'd love to captain Leicester if the opportunity ever arose. I did captain Newbold Colts, Coventry Colts and Warwickshire Under-21s so I'm not inexperienced, but I'm sure people would probably smirk at such a suggestion. 'Christ, the way he behaves and the way he plays? No way can he captain Leicester!' I can hear them saying. I think you don't know how the individual will react until you actually put him into the specific situation. I believe I possess several valuable qualities that would be of benefit to the team, both in the way I play and in my loyalty to the players and the club. Against that, there are several other big names at the club who would doubtless be preferred. My feeling is the club could do a lot worse than take a punt on me.

The captaincy of England is more about public relations than anything else. If you can handle the press well, as Lawrence Dallaglio did, you've cracked it. That's the key. Of course, you must also be an automatic first choice, as Lawrence and Johnno are. When I played under Phil de Glanville's captaincy out in Argentina, he was the first-choice centre – and he was an effective skipper, albeit in a different way to Lawrence and Johnno. That's because he's a back, and not suprisingly his mentality differs from that of a forward. When a back is the captain he invariably wants the ball to be spread to the backs, whereas a forward captain, to a certain degree, prefers it the other way round. Phil doesn't shout – he's very calm and doesn't need foul language to make his point, which forwards tend to do. It's the nature of the beast, isn't it? Phil respects his forwards, though, and treats them like adults. He'll merely say: 'You know the job you've got to do, just go out and do it.' You can't tell someone how to play when you don't know that position, and Phil knows how far to take things before leaving matters to the individual player. The captain's input, whoever he is, whether at club or international level, is still quite limited for the simple reason that the game plan, for want of a better phrase, has been formulated by the coaches.

A lot is made about the importance of having game plans. Most of the time they're just a load of bullshit. You play to your strengths and to the opposition's weaknesses, that's all there is to it. Leicester are criticised for being a forwards-dominated side. Yes, we have a good pack of forwards: why acknowledge such a strength and then ignore it? If I was a coach I'd build my team round a set of forwards because that's the way I've always played and that's how I think the game should be played. Forwards win games, don't they? Backs just decide by how much. We don't have any particular game plans. The forwards win the ball and the backs get it whenever they want it. If Joel Stransky didn't want the ball, he'd leave it to us to do the job he knew we were capable of. People think about the game too much. It's dead simple, really. If they've got a weak set of forwards, you batter them up front; if their backs are weak, you allow yours to run at them as much as possible. Admittedly, the coaches will have identified these strengths and weaknesses for us by extensive study of videos: the back of the lineout; the blind side of scrums; the wingers lie too flat, leaving space behind; wingers hanging too deep, leaving space outside the centres; the fly-half drifting across too quickly, leaving holes in that channel; they may be susceptible to drives from the lineout. You might uncover three or four areas to exploit in any particular game and you concentrate on those throughout the week and take them into the game that weekend. You can't become too bogged down on the subject of game plans and their implementation. It's not rocket science we're dealing with here, is it?

Coaches are important in the sense that we play in the style they want us to play, having provided us with the equipment to do so. Some are strong on technique, others strong on motivation. Whatever the case, there are certain qualities which the players tend to look for in a coach. Probably most important of all, the coach must know precisely what he wants and where he wants to go; he should then stick to his principles and not change his mind from one day to the next. Secondly, he must know how to get the best out of his men. You can take the best 15 players in the world, but if they don't get on with the coach, or they think he's doing things wrong and they're reluctant to follow his route, the team won't perform to its potential. It just ain't gonna happen!

I don't think it's necessary to have been a top player yourself in order to gain the respect of the guys in your charge but I do believe the individual has to be extra special to make it as a top coach if he hasn't done it himself on the field, because otherwise players will give him a lot less time to establish himself. If you're Joel Stransky, John Wells, Andy Robinson or Rob Andrew, for example, the players will give you more leeway. They know you've done the things you're talking about. You tend to receive instant respect in these circumstances. Otherwise, players may say, 'What do you know about it? You've never played at this level. I have. Why should you know better than me?' It's only to be expected, really.

When the coach has a player's respect he will be listened to. Some of the things a coach may say to me could be utter nonsense but I'll listen all the same. There might be the odd point here and there that is valid and I'll take it on board. Even if there is nothing valid, it's important from both the coach's and the player's point of view that you do listen since it gives both sides the impression they are being appreciated. That way, at least, everyone thinks they're having a say in what is going on. I don't think it works if coaches just lay down the law. Players must have a bit of power. The coach must keep them happy. They have to be friendly, though not over-familiar, because if you're in charge you can't become too friendly or the relationship will break down. The coach is the disciplinarian; occasionally he has to break bad news. He must stay aloof and apart to a certain extent, although not so much as to create a them-and-us situation, which would only cause the players to dislike him. At the end of the day, players want to be treated as equals. They need to feel their opinions matter, that the coach might use them to fine-tune his basic philosophies as to how the game should be played. What the players don't want is a coach who says 'Do this', and who, when they ask 'Why?', says 'Do it!'. That is a recipe for disaster.

The appointment of Australia's World Cup-winning coach Bob Dwyer was the best thing that could have happened to Leicester at the dawn of the professional era. Bob and his assistant, the former Australian lock Duncan Hall, were totally different to anybody I'd experienced before. Bob showed us so much that was new, not just in terms of playing the game out on the pitch but throughout the entire set-up – training schedules, facilities, diet, conditioning. He established a fantastic structure at the club, everyone would agree with that – even his biggest enemies at Welford Road – and a lot of what we do now is what we did with Bob. He took every player out of his comfort zone and made him a better player – and I mean *every* player at the club. Perhaps as a technical coach Bob wasn't the best, but he was quite a motivator in the way he spoke to players and conducted himself. His enthusiasm for the game was immense. Dunc was not much of a talker in comparison but he possessed a great depth of knowledge and his coaching of scrums and lineouts was tremendously detailed. They were a good combination. Bob knew how he wanted to play the game and the players he wanted. He didn't go into an awful lot of detail about how things should be done. He left that to the guys he appointed to oversee each area.

I think Dean Richards was instrumental in getting Bob removed. Dean's body was wearing out towards the end and I don't think he – or Wellsy, who was in the same boat – took kindly to being pushed aside. Perhaps Bob was getting a little too big for his boots at the club, too powerful for some people's liking. It wasn't Bob's fault. If you keep giving someone rope, he's going to take it until it's stretched as far as it'll go, isn't he? Perhaps the club should have put its foot down a little earlier. When Bob was appointed, our old coach, Ian 'Dosser' Smith, was meant to stay on as his assistant but Bob said he didn't want him, he preferred Duncan Hall. The club had just given Dosser a contract and now he'd no job. They had to find something for him to do, which was ridiculous. Bob was just an employee of the club, like me or Peter Wheeler, but instead of telling him, 'This is your assistant coach,' they let him rule the roost. Eventually, the club began to lose control over Bob and that's why he was sacked, in my opinion. I know team spirit was going down the pan a little and we'd lost our way on the pitch by our standards – all of which Dean, who was still active on the playing side, undoubtedly conveyed to the members of the board with whom he is very friendly, people like Dave Matthews, Bob Beason, Pete Tom and Roy Jackson. Dean may well have been chipping away at Bob's position and ultimately the board decided it had to do something about the situation.

Dean was the board's get-out clause when Bob and Dunc were sacked. If the board had appointed John Wells as coach assisted by Joel Stransky to do the backs, everyone would have said they'd never cope. Because the fans love Dean so much for what he's done for the club, he would be viewed as a saviour, the messiah, who would get us out of the shit – supposed shit – we were in at the time. Dean's such an influential figure that his appointment would be acceptable; he saved the board a lot of embarrassment. Dean does no coaching whatsoever. I think the club created his role of manager to keep him at Leicester. I don't know that for a fact, but that's the way I see it. Dean has found it more difficult to adapt to his new job than either Wellsy or Joel. Those who know Dean can see his personality is not the type you'd associate with being the manager of a rugby team. He finds it very difficult to talk to people at times, especially if the situation is an awkward one. But he does possess some valuable attributes: he does a wonderful amount of PR for the club and he's an excellent judge of character in rugby-playing terms. As a manager running the side, though, I think the team would function just as efficiently without him. I may be wrong. Dean is a great guy and a good friend, but I think if you asked him yourself he'd admit he's found it quite difficult to find his feet in this new role – simply because he'd rather still be out on the pitch doing things instead of sitting behind a desk covered with piles of paperwork and having to talk to people.

Dean has taken a lot of credit for what has happened since Bob's departure in the spring of 1998, but none of it would have happened without John Wells. It's not down to Dean that we won the Premiership in 1998–99. Wellsy turned things round for us. He listened to the players, used some opinions and trashed others, and because he's very inexperienced in coaching terms, he concentrates on the basics – which is the way he played. We scrum, we ruck, we maul, we lineout, we tackle, we pass and we catch for hours on end. If you do the simple things well, you won't go far wrong. Occasionally, coaches fall into the trap of becoming too fancy with regard to what we're going to do with the ball. They get sidetracked and forget the crux of the game, which revolves around winning the ball at scrum, lineout and in contact situations.

I must admit to being surprised at how Wellsy has turned out. I didn't think he would become a very good coach because he is not exactly very outgoing, the life and soul of the party or a great socialiser. During the first few months in charge, he was very schoolmasterish in the way he dealt with us, clearly wanting to be seen as in control. Looking back, I can appreciate why he behaved like this: he needed to establish his authority quickly, having been promoted from the playing side. At the time, though, I thought it was never going to work, that it was hopeless. Wellsy has proved me wrong. He has a very good rugby brain and puts his thoughts across well; the players work hard for him because they respect him from his playing days; and he's come on a ton. For example, Wellsy will still come and talk to me about scrummaging, to learn what goes on in the front row. He's keen to gather other players' experiences, and he learns very quickly. Whether he would be as good a coach at another club where he had to start off not knowing anybody is another question. I think he might find that more difficult. By knowing everybody at Leicester, it was easier for him to make the transition from player to coach, but once he's got a few more years under his belt, there's a good chance Wellsy could be an excellent coach at any club.

One of Wellsy's trump cards is the fact that he doesn't have an ego problem. Whereas Bob Dwyer and Austin Healey were at each other's throats because they both had very large egos, Wellsy won't rise to the bait. If Austin – or anyone else for that matter – wants to cross swords with him, he won't bother arguing during training. He'll just see the individual afterwards and tell him that if he doesn't want to be part of the team he should leave Leicester. There's no arguing the toss. People know where they stand as a result. Austin can't mess around; I can't mess around; no one can. You cannot afford to give players a forum in which to argue. They must either conform and do as they're told, fit the Leicester mould as it were, or they must be told they can go. I feel, for instance, that Bob gave Austin too much opportunity to talk – there was too much scope for debate. Someone has to be the boss, like him or lump him. We know Wellsy is the gaffer and he has the final say on most things. He'll accommodate your opinions and a compromise may be sought, but his word is then law. Then it's either come into line or leave.

As a result, it's a pretty happy ship at Leicester at the moment. The players all want to be there. If Bob had stayed, for example,

I'm sure Austin would not be at the club. From my sources I think I can say without fear of contradiction that Bob would have got rid of him. These days Austin is on a stickier wicket because Wellsy is liked by so many people and is held in so much respect within the club that to cross him would be fatal. It was perhaps always easier to 'Judas' Bob because he was an outsider who was going to be at Leicester for three years, take the money and go. That's no criticism of Bob – that's the nature of the business he's in. All in all, more loyalty is liable to be shown Dean and Wellsy.

Having foreign coaches is like having foreign players. They're here for only a short period. If you start relying on them too much, what happens when they're gone? Who's going to replace Joel now he's finished? Admittedly it was an injury which brought his time to an end but he surely wouldn't have stayed for too long. Joel will probably take to coaching a lot better than Wellsy did. He's a more outgoing person and, as a former playmaker, he probably understands the game a whole lot better. Wellsy was a blind-side flanker and never had to make all that many decisions on how the game was to be played. Foreign players are valuable because we can learn so much from them, but to rely on them is very dangerous. You need their quality, but as much as I like guys like Joel, Waisale Serevi, Fritz van Heerden, Pat Howard and Dave Lougheed, I'd much prefer to have 15 Englishmen in the side, since there's a greater likelihood they will remain year after year. You can't have a continual chain of bought-in players. It's preferable to get a local lad and turn him into a Joel or a Fritz – like the club did with Johnno, Backy, Matt Poole and the three of us in the front row – and keep him for ten years. Someone like Lewis Moody will possibly play his entire career at Leicester; Adam Balding has come over from Coventry; Paul Gustard is virtually an honorary Leicester boy now. It just won't work if you rely on foreigners – players or coaches – coming in every two or three years.

At the time I didn't agree with the board's decision to terminate Bob's contract. Now, with the benefit of hindsight, it appears the best thing the club could have done. Whether that was very sound judgement on the part of the board or more luck than judgement – I think it was more the latter, although the board will take the credit – is more debatable. However, the credit should go to Wellsy and the players who've done all the graft.

Of all the coaches I've worked with I'd have to say that Dosser Smith made the most impact on me. When I came from Coventry to Leicester in 1992, at the age of 21, and saw the passion that Dosser had for Leicester, it made an immense impression on me. He instilled in all his players the qualities of Leicester and the commitment they should show to the club. I was completely uncontrollable at times and some people considered me a liability. Dosser stuck with me through thick and thin. He'd pull me to one side and encourage me to stay the same essentially but channel my aggression to better purpose. He recognised my worth and was prepared to tolerate the flawed side of my personality. He believed in me. If some had had their way, I would not have stayed in the first team. Thanks to Dosser, my detractors were kept off my back.

There's no doubt Dosser was the heart and soul of Leicester Tigers when he was coach in the early 1990s. How he would fare coaching in the Premiership today, I don't know for sure. He coaches and plays the game in quite an old-fashioned way for these days – though to be fair he's never had the opportunity to prove himself. Still, perhaps he has a better rugby brain than many people think, because he saw my potential and, thankfully, I've been able to live up to his expectations to a certain degree. I am grateful for the faith he showed in me, which brought me safely through some tricky situations. Dosser said many things which switched me on. They made me tick. Dosser will always have my respect.

ELEVEN

THE MONEY GAME

PROFESSIONAL rugby is my chance to escape from the rat race. We earn pretty good money, though not mega amounts. I certainly couldn't live off my rugby earnings forever. But I've a nice house; I've invested in a property which I rent out; I've put some money into various pensions and PEPs. I've done what I can to make myself reasonably financially secure by the time I finish playing – which will probably be in seven years or so when I'm 35. I know that I'll have to work again at something or other, but at least I'll be able to do what I want to do without worrying where every penny is going to come from.

I once read in the papers that I earn £140,000 to £160,000 a year from Leicester and England. That's just a fantasy! Something around £100,000 is more like it, if I play for both. Each member of the England World Cup squad was on a retainer of £1,750 a month for four months, plus match fees. In the Five Nations it's £3,000 to play plus a £1,500 win bonus; for southern-hemisphere games it's £3,000 to play and £3,000 to win. Playing includes sitting on the bench, even if you don't get on the pitch –

which is fair, because everyone has done the same work leading up to the game. That way you avoid a two-tier system developing.

People tend to get too carried away on the subject of money. I can appreciate why the general public are interested in what celebrities earn, although their fascination can become both puzzling and frustrating. If you're a businessman who has made money, for example, people congratulate you for becoming a success, but if you make your money from sport a lot of people seem to resent it. I can't understand their thinking. They say I have a great life, playing sport, travelling the world, getting paid handsomely for it. That's quite true and I wouldn't swap my job. However, there's a lot of hard work involved, the body takes a hell of a battering, and our commitment is extraordinarily high compared to some professional sports. If anything, professional rugby players deserve *more* money but in the current financial climate you get what you produce. That's why we have agents. They are a necessary evil. You must have an agent or how else do you discover how to price yourself? Agents shop around and find out your market value. The fact that I play for Leicester helps sell season tickets. If I'm capped, the agent merchandises my increased profile. You don't want to be greedy but you must realise your worth and maximise your potential. For instance, Mizuno pay me to wear their boots, giving me £4,000 a season and £300 per international; and a Leicester-based firm, Zero One One Six, sponsor me to the tune of £4,000 a season, which goes to the club and helps pay my salary.

Take my contract with Leicester, for another example. I had a contract with the club which I think, from memory, gave me a retainer of £22,000 plus match fees of £250 to play and £250 to win during the first professional season of 1996–97. On the face of it, good money. But I found out that I was being paid only a half or a third as much as some players of similar ability and experience at other clubs. In other words, I was being paid well below my market value. I was happy at Leicester and didn't want to leave – unless it was for extraordinary circumstances. I was an international by this stage, but renegotiating my contract in the summer of 1997, the club offered £40,000, flat rate, to stay – with no provision for appearance money or win bonuses. This looked an obvious improvement on the previous season's figure until I realised that with all the matches I'd played my earnings had been around £42,000. In theory I was facing a pay cut.

I knew quite a lot of the Northampton players, and the next thing I know, Keith Barwell, the Saints' owner, is on the phone: do Graham, Darren and I fancy a move? In the meantime, Tim Buttimore, my agent and a former Tigers player, had been to see Bob Dwyer. Bob told him the club could get a Super 12 player for £25,000 so why should it pay more for me? The club refused to budge. I thought, if that's what they're going to give me in return for four to five years' loyalty when I stayed instead of moving elsewhere, in addition to underpaying me by twenty or thirty grand, I may as well go. Keith Barwell offered me £50,000 tax paid, cash in hand if I wanted, just to sign, plus a contract worth fifty to sixty grand on top: to him I was worth £100,000, while to Leicester I was replaceable for £25,000.

All three of us were ready to go – not wanting to particularly, but professional rugby is a business. It's a short career and you've got to make the most of it. Basically, the club were ripping us off and we weren't happy about it. Eventually they came back with a deal that was more acceptable: a £40,000 retainer plus £500 per game and £500 for a win, with 20 of the match fees guaranteed.

This was not as much as I would have earned at Northampton – let alone the extra fifty grand I'd have had in the bank – but I didn't want to leave Leicester. The three of us wanted to stay with the fans and with our mates. We wanted to stay loyal to them.

I can appreciate the fact that Peter Wheeler and Bob Dwyer were trying to get us as cheap as they could – that's business – and some people may think we were being greedy by asking for more. However, to be quite honest, I would have left had the club not revised their offer, simply because I felt they were showing me no loyalty. They were getting players in – not only foreigners – and paying them twice as much as me, yet I'd been there five years and they knew my pedigree, knew I could do the job, had won cups and the league and had red, white and green blood running through my veins. This scenario demonstrated how deeply the professional mentality has permeated Leicester. They want the best players and if you're not doing it for them, they'll get rid of you. Players like Rory Underwood, John Liley, Jez Harris, Steve Hackney, Aadel Kardooni and Niall Malone have all departed. Those guys were the mainstays of the club when the game was amateur. Even Bob Dwyer and Duncan Hall had to go in the end.

It would have broken our hearts to leave but you have to do what's best for yourself and your family. Loyalty doesn't pay the mortgage, the bills or contribute to the pension fund. I feel strongly that the club should reward those players who served Leicester well over a long period of time, people like the three of us in the front row, Johnno, Matt Poole, Backy, Stuart Potter and Jamie Hamilton. We've produced the goods week in, week out for a number of years. I felt bitter that players had come in and were being paid more than me even though the club didn't know whether they'd stay, how long they'd stay or whether they could actually do it for the team. I don't blame the players who came to Leicester – it was good business sense from their standpoint. The club's explanation was that you must pay more money to attract players into Leicester. Why? If you want to buy an English hooker it'll cost you twice as much as I'm being paid under the new contract. I accepted the revised offer because I was happy at Leicester and didn't want to leave. But it could have gone horribly wrong for the club. The front row is the core of the team: the infamous ABC Club. When you forfeit the spirit – the culture even – that we three instil, you lose something unique. Had Darren, Graham and I left, I think the club would have been set on a downward spiral and would not have been as successful as they subsequently were. That may be an arrogant way of looking at it, but I think it's the honest truth. I think Dean realised that, which is why he's gone back to basics more than perhaps Bob did. He realises that getting the fundamentals right has always been the crux of Leicester's method and resultant success.

Of course, some people will be adamant that we are overpaid for the little we are supposed to do. They say we don't train very much or very often. Well, during the season, Thursday is the only day we get off, and that's a day your partner is probably at work herself, so any normal domestic life is destroyed. Even on a Sunday we have to go down to the gym in the morning for a post-match recovery session – a swim, a jacuzzi, cycling and so on. We don't do it as a team but I'll probably meet up informally with a few of the boys, and our wives and girlfriends will join us for their own workout. Otherwise it's a case of the rugby widows syndrome because Sunday afternoon is the only other time you'll have together.

I enjoy all forms of training. Once you're match fit it becomes relatively easy. Winter training can be a pain, though, when the pitches are muddy, the wind is howling and the rain is pissing down. Fitness work and grafting in those conditions can be taxing. But it ain't that bad – especially if you're winning. If you're losing, it feels like something else altogether!

Monday morning means weights at Oval Park for a couple of hours, followed by rugby training in the afternoon. Lunch is provided at the training ground, something with pasta, rice or baked potatoes. We do have to watch our diet. Crisps, chocolate, anything high in fat with little in the way of nutrition, must be avoided. The days of ale, fried food and McDonald's are out of the window. No more Guinness and bacon sandwiches for Daz – I always said he used to cut the fat off his bacon and make another sandwich out of that! I suppose you might lapse once every six weeks or so, but basically we know that if it tastes great, it's bad for you. It's a change of lifestyle which is good for you, though, because you're eating healthier food. I stuck to it even on my honeymoon, out in Australia after our summer training camp finished. I had a training schedule and put in one and a half hours every day of the two weeks. In that time – on the coast near Cairns – I ate one ice-cream and the only alcohol to pass my lips was one glass of wine with my evening meal. I knew that back home there were three blokes after my job and they weren't on holiday! You cannot relax your discipline. The other Saturday, for instance, Sarah-Jane and I went down the pub to meet some friends for food. They were all there drinking lager and vodka and Coke on a hot summer evening, while I had to sit there holding an orange juice and soda water. A couple of lovely cold lagers was out of the question. Eventually I couldn't stand it any longer and went home. I left Sarah-Jane enjoying herself and said I'd pick her up later. The temptation was becoming too great. I went home and watched television till 11.30. It's a wrench, yes, but I'd sacrifice all the food and drink in the world just to run out at Twickenham the once, let alone 20-odd times.

Tuesday tends to be the same as Monday; Wednesday will be only one session, rugby, probably in the afternoon; Thursday is free; Friday will be a team-run in the morning and travelling in the afternoon if it is an away game on the Saturday. This routine can become monotonous, especially if you're on a losing streak. You have to keep reminding yourself it's a damn sight better than going into the workshop every day like I used to, or heading for an office. I love the fact that I live in a tracksuit rather than a collar and tie. You even get used to all the travelling, which is no more arduous than that of a salesman. I usually share most of the driving with Graham.

Friday is always an early night, in bed by ten or half-past. I never have a problem sleeping before a match – it's Saturday morning that is the problem. Throughout the morning I like to remain focused on the afternoon ahead. I don't want to be sidetracked. I don't like anyone talking to me. I only want to think and get into game mode. I try to keep out of the way of Sarah-Jane. I'll get up at nine and eat breakfast as soon as I can, cereal and toast, that's all. I'll eat again, around midday, probably beans on toast, making sure I take in plenty of fluid, water or Lucozade, throughout the morning.

For a match at Welford Road kicking off at three, we'll meet in one of the units at the ground at one o'clock. The forwards and backs will separate to begin with. We'll discuss what we're going to do, what they're likely to do and what we're going to do about it. The team then comes together for a final chat before we move off to the changing-room at 1.30 p.m. We warm up at 2.25 p.m. so you've got 55 minutes in between to kill. Some of the guys, like Fritz van Heerden, will actually go to sleep. I might read the programme, strap up anything that happens to be knackered, have a walk on the pitch, although I tend to get changed quickly. Before we had Next as our sponsor and began to warm up in their T-shirts, I used to warm up in my playing kit – it didn't matter if it was raining or muddy. I liked to go out and get it shitted up straightaway. If it was left to me I'd make everyone put their match kit on straight off. It's going to get dirty anyway, isn't it? By now some of the boys might be laughing and joking, a bit relaxed or maybe just plain nervous. I'll give them some abuse to get them into game mode, make them tense and into the same frame of mind as me. Each to their own, though. As I've got older I've learnt to accommodate other people's methods. Not that I can understand people who sit in the changing-room all quiet. I don't know what makes them tick. It certainly doesn't work for me. Our warm-up consists of a few drills, lineouts, mauling, some hits on the tackle bags. Then, with ten minutes to go, it's back into the changing-room. Johnno will have a few words and, more than likely, so will I. I'll remind people of their responsibilities, tell them how crap the opposition are, that nothing matters more than this, you're playing for Leicester – don't worry about playing for England next week, forget it. So, by the time we get out there, we've developed a fair hatred for the team we're playing against.

The tension in the changing-room immediately before you go out can be so intense it's almost impossible to describe. You're so afraid of failure, of not winning, of letting yourself and your team-mates down. You've all this nervous energy coursing through your body, waiting to be channelled into hitting the first scrum or first tackle or first ruck. Once you do that, the nerves vanish because you're in an environment you're prepared for. The playing side is the easy part – it's the psychological side of thinking about the game that you're less trained to deal with satisfactorily. I remember how nervous I was in my first season at Leicester before we ran out to play Northampton in the semi-final of the 1992–93 Pilkington Cup. In their pack they had Buck Shelford, the All Black, and England internationals like Gary Pearce, Martin Bayfield, Tim Rodber and John Olver at hooker. It was all new to me. Playing in a cup final was the height of my ambition at the time. We destroyed them 28–6 and went on to beat Harlequins 23–16 in the final. Nevertheless, the most nervous dressing-room of the lot as far as I'm concerned was Old Trafford before the New Zealand Test of 1997. The fear factor was enormous that day. It was an extra crap, extra puke, elephants in the gut!

The adrenaline rush you get running out at Welford Road or Twickenham is fantastic. You'll do anything for the team at that moment. I always go out second. I'd lead the side out if they'd let me because I just want to get out there and get started. I always run out. Some like to walk out slowly. Dean never ran out, but he didn't like running, full stop! Some teams will be waiting for us on the pitch, eyeballing us. That really gets on my tits and makes me want to get in their faces even more. We'll huddle up and, if the opposition has been eyeballing us, we'll use that as last-second motivation. 'Who do they think they are, trying that on our pitch?' We've created a winning attitude at Welford Road: our patch, our fortress, no one comes here and f***s us about. We pride ourselves on being unbeatable at Welford Road.

Winning is expected. The coaches expect us to win. The fans expect us to win. *We* expect to win. It's as simple as that.

Afterwards it's not so much a feeling of elation or satisfaction as a sense of relief at the end of a tough week's work. You just want to have a bath, shave and have a drink. It's only the crunch games that yield real enjoyment: beating Newcastle 21–12 away to win the 1998–99 Premiership and Richmond 23–11 away in midweek when we don't play so well midweek. Winning is everything. You get your bonus, you get your points, the fans are happy. But we also want to perform, because we've worked so hard during the week. We have high standards. We want to do ourselves justice in front of the fans. When you've trained hard, watched your diet, avoided the booze and played your guts out on a Saturday, only the highest level of performance generates that special buzz.

The Leicester fans are used to success. In that regard they are fickle because nothing less is acceptable. The good thing about this mentality is that the players know what they're in for from the outset and that only their best is going to be good enough. The fans don't mind how we play or how well we play so long as we win. They appreciate all styles of rugby at Welford Road. We can grind out a victory in the pouring rain using the forwards and the fans are just as happy as if we've run in ten tries on a sunny afternoon. They're fickle in the sense that they want us to be successful but they're not fickle about the manner in which success is achieved. The players echo that mentality. If we must play nine-man rugby to win a game, we'll do it and enjoy doing it. The fans soon let us know if they're unhappy, even more so nowadays because they're paying two or three times as much to watch us as they did in the amateur days. They have every right to make their feelings known. They are, without a doubt, the finest fans in the country. They follow us everywhere; at away matches we frequently have more support than the home team.

Training with England in the week leading up to an international at Twickenham, for example, is slightly different. We meet up on the Monday afternoon or Tuesday morning at the Petersham Hotel. The sessions are much shorter and more intense than any at Oval Park. We'll usually train just once a day, with all the heavy stuff – scrummaging, rucking, tackling – early in the week so that you can recover. On Thursday we'll have a team-run in the afternoon, with lineouts and possibly half a dozen scrums to retain our focus. Friday will be a walk through in the morning, that's all; Saturday morning we'll go through a few lineouts. There's not an awful lot of chat on the training pitch. At this level you don't tend to say anything, even if someone is doing things you think are wrong. You're not there for long – do you rock the boat and upset a few people? At Leicester we have a certain way of doing things which we instil in players when they arrive. If they don't like it, they may as well leave because they're not going to fit in. At club level you're more honest with each other than you are in the international set-up. If people drop out of training or if they're always in the medical room they tend to get some verbals. As you see each other every day it has to be like that or else it would drive you mad – whereas at international level you let things pass because you know you're not going to be together in a few days' time. An international week can, in fact, become rather tedious. You tend to stay in during the evenings, watching videos or playing pool, although some of the London-based guys will go home. It's a quiet life. But there's a job to be done, isn't there?

One problem with the game today for international players is that you hardly ever get a summer off to recharge your batteries. I've played rugby all year round since 1996, and last summer's Australian Test was my fortieth game of the season – and it's not as if many of those were low-key friendlies. They were all high-performance games which take a lot out of you. In three years I've had just three weeks out of training. I can't complain, though. I've signed a contract with England, and I get paid very well for it. You can't sign a contract and then moan about how hard you're working. That's part of the deal. If you think it's going to be too much for you, don't sign the contract, don't take the money and don't do it.

Having said that, it's not the number of games that causes the trouble as much as the lack of opportunity to rest, recuperate and build up your body. Playing is in some ways the easy part. It's all the preparation which takes the toll, especially with England, which is intense enough without all the demands from the media. It's not difficult to end up both physically and mentally drained. You may get a few niggles, have treatment and play through them instead of resting, all of which wears you down mentally. I've had problems with my back ever since I joined Leicester in 1992. I got into such a state with chronic backache and sciatica in my legs that I was forced to have a scan, which showed my bottom two discs had prolapsed and were crunched up. I was only 22! My body does take a helluva pounding. Sometimes the day after a game I can't bend down to put my socks on, or I can't look round because I'm so stiff-shouldered. If you're whacking your spine from top to bottom 40 times a game, you are going to end up feeling like an ironing board. The public don't always appreciate what we put out bodies through. It's the rough, tough stuff we're getting paid for, all the training and getting your body smashed up from time to time; taking anti-inflammatories so you can play the next day; having six injections of local anaesthetics around popped rib cartilages 20 minutes before kick-off in order to kill the pain – and then having to scrummage on those ribs so when you wake up the following morning they're twice as sore. A lot of junior club players also smash their bodies in the same way and I hold my hands up to them because they're not being paid or receiving the kind of excellent medical attention that us professionals get. But I bet not many of the critics who think we are lucky and overpaid would wish to trade places with me on those painful occasions.

Rugby, particularly with England, is a means to an end. You're only in it for a short time and you must make the most of it while you can. That's what keeps you sane when the pressure is on and the world seems to be spinning out of control: you're getting a good wedge. Take it and take the shit that comes with it. In a few years' time, when I've finished, it'll be someone else's turn to go through it.

TWELVE

PREPARING FOR THE BIG ONE

IN many eyes, England's preparations for the World Cup were overshadowed by the Dallaglio 'affair' – the allegations made in a Sunday tabloid that the England captain had taken recreational drugs on the 1997 Lions tour to South Africa and had once, in his youth, been a drug dealer.

The party line on Lawrence amongst the squad was that we were all behind him. We were allowed to speak to the press on the issue if we wanted to – in no way were we gagged – but the guy was in a very sticky situation. Do you hammer the last nail into his coffin or do you support him? You never know what sort of situation you'll end up in yourself. I'd like to think that if I were in any kind of similar situation the guys would take the same line. To persecute a guy because he's done something that perhaps he shouldn't have done is a bit harsh.

Lawrence got shafted big-time. Whatever he said to these undercover reporters and whatever he did in the past, he was stitched up; 95 per cent of the story is probably a load of bollocks. Lawrence is a good fella, with a lovely girlfriend, Alice, and two kids. Our first reaction was to think of them – they are the ones who suffer – and his mum and his dad. Yes, he was stupid but he's not the one who will really suffer. He's big enough to look after himself. He lost the captaincy – and he was a good skipper – but Johnno is no bad substitute, is he? Johnno was just matter-of-fact about it: this has happened to Lawrence; there's nothing we can do about it; we might as well get on with the job.

To be fair to Lawrence, as soon as the story broke he went straight round to Clive Woodward's house and resigned as captain. He could have hung on to it and let the RFU or Clive give him the sack. He knew it would be detrimental to the team to try and stay on as captain, so he didn't try to hold on and blag his way out of it; he resigned and said he'd sort it out. He forfeited an awful lot. He's gone from being very much involved with selection and everything we do, to being one of the foot soldiers once again. He's taken it on the chin.

Lawrence was obviously a little bit concerned with the outcome of the inquiry, but there was no evidence against him on the principal charge of taking recreational drugs. He was never going to get off scot-free because probably he had 'brought the game into disrepute' and, quite simply, the RFU can't be seen to have taken no action. That's the way the RFU tend to be. In any other country – Australia, New Zealand, South Africa – he'd have been cleared and back playing in an instant because those countries want their players to play. Here we seem to think for some reason that we must do the English thing and go through the motions. There was no proof. They were just dragging the matter out. In the end he was fined £15,000 and £10,000 costs, plus his own legal costs of, allegedly, £75,000. It was the end of a sorry saga we were all glad to see the back of. It was becoming a distraction. It was all the press wanted to talk about and it wasn't fair to the rest of the squad, especially the newcomers, because Lawrence was hogging the limelight and stealing their chance of some publicity – which annoyed Lawrence because he is very much a team man.

Are there drugs – recreational or otherwise – in rugby? I've been involved in senior rugby for ten years and during those ten years I've never seen any type of drug abuse, of any sort, in any sphere, at any club I've been to, or any gym I've trained at. I've no doubt there is drug abuse going on somewhere, but where isn't there drug abuse in our society today? I'm sure there are office workers, factory workers and so on doing drugs because the problem is everywhere. People say steroid abuse is rife in rugby. That's complete and utter rubbish. If you look at the guys in the English game, there are not many you could say have changed shape massively over a 12-month period. If anything, our guys, especially the backs, are a little small, and you can't say any of our forwards are exceptionally huge. Certain ex-players say it's rife but what hard evidence do they come up with? They just want to grab some headlines, don't they?

Several players, it's true, have been caught with banned substances in their system. They have gone to disciplinary hearings and the negative test is invariably found to be the result of taking cold remedies or something like that, which, if you take large amounts, act as a pick-me-up. I don't know of any rugby player who has taken such remedies to enhance their performance. The drug testers themselves also have a responsibility to get it right because, as in the Diane Modahl case, they can sometimes get it very wrong.

All the England squad had to sign forms agreeing to be tested for drugs at any time, 24 hours a day, seven days a week. I received a phone call at home at 8.40 one morning from the International Olympic Committee, who conduct all the testing over here, to say I'd been picked out for a random test and would have to give a urine sample within 24 hours. Their guy turned up at 11 a.m., explained the procedure, did the paperwork and asked me to pee in a couple of pots. That was that. If you take drugs it's going to kill you, so I don't think the possibility even crosses the minds of most guys in the game.

Our preparations for the World Cup began out in Australia in June, where we played two games, against Queensland and Australia, during a three-week training camp based at Couran Cove on South Stradbroke Island, which is off Surfers Paradise, near Brisbane. This was an awesome place, designed by the former world record distance runner Ron Clarke, set amid beaches and rainforests and complete with wallabies jumping around everywhere and snakes under your feet. The accommodation was superb, as were the facilities – a full gymnasium, running tracks and Olympic-size swimming-pool – since it was meant to be a leisure complex for holidaymakers. The camp wasn't exactly quite what we expected, however. We'd all had a hard season – I'd played 38 games, for example – and we were led to believe the first ten days would be rest and recovery, getting your body back together again, that sort of thing. Because I'd just got married I arrived a day late, along with Daz and Wig, who'd acted as ushers – but after a 24-hour flight and checking in at 11 a.m., we were out on a four-mile run in the afternoon! The next morning it was up at seven for protein shakes, before weight training at 7.30 a.m. for one and a half hours, followed by breakfast and on to the rugby field by 10.30 a.m.

The stay was pretty uneventful. Training saw the odd punch-up, but nothing more than that. Daz gave Trevor Woodman a shiner one day, and Trevor stuck the nut straight on him in response. The occasional feisty session is almost encouraged. As long as what happens on the training field stays there and isn't allowed to develop into a vendetta, it's fine. Off the pitch, things were equally peaceful. There was nowhere to socialise, not even a bar, and we were too tired most of the time anyway. We did have one night out in Surfers Paradise, but that's all. The State of Origin rugby league was on television, which was definitely high-octane stuff, but apart from that we didn't get up to much. Some of the boys water-skiied and jet-skiied, and went sea fishing – but I get seasick so I gave that a miss.

We trained more with the World Cup in mind than the two games we were due to play in Australia. We had a good result against Queensland, winning 39–14 (although to be fair to Queensland they did have a lot of players ruled out through being in the Wallabies squad) considering we'd not played for several weeks and were understandably rusty. We began the Australia Test very well but if you give the Wallabies chances to score they will take them. From being 7–0 up and in charge, we were suddenly 10–7 down and they were back in the game. We ran out of steam after that and lost 22–15 – but they were in the middle of their season and we'd not played for five weeks or so.

We reconvened on 25 July at the Royal Marine Commando Training Centre in Lympstone, Devon, for three days of intensive activities designed to test our decision-making ability under extreme pressure. Apart from telling us the Marines were in charge on the first morning, Woody had no input. We were also very much in the dark. We knew we'd be going over the assault course and yomping across Dartmoor, but the Marines don't tell you anything in advance, only when you need to know it – which is a minute before you're going to do it! In the army, whoever's in charge commands, and those of lower rank obey. That way you're kept very mentally alert because you never know what's coming next.

We should have guessed we were in for some nasty surprises when we turned up on the Sunday. Martin Corry, Graham Rowntree and I arrived at the main gate to be greeted by the highest security – guys with shooters all over the gate. We gave our names and were told to wait while they got a 'runner' for us: this young soldier, togged out in all the kit, runs in front of our car, directing us to the officers' mess, where we were staying. They can't walk anywhere! We thought, 'Christ! What have we got into here?'

Naturally, we harboured reservations that we'd get absolutely 'beasted': a load of jumped-up army guys abusing us for three days. As it turned out, they were outstanding blokes. We were in awe of them because they'd served in Northern Ireland, Iraq, Bosnia or wherever, and been in several life-threatening situations – and yet, to a certain extent, they were in awe of us because we'd played rugby for England. There was a lot of mutual respect. Socially, we wanted to talk to them and discover what they'd done in their army lives; all they wanted to talk about was our rugby careers. Staying in the officers' mess was luxurious five-star accommodation compared to the billets of the other lads. We had a cabin apiece, complete with bed, desk, wardrobe, sink, plus shared toilet and shower – the bed was tiny but you worked so hard during the day you couldn't care less what it was like by the time you fell into it.

Monday morning began at seven with a knock on the door. I opened it to find a chap standing there holding a cup of tea. I thought it had to be one of the lads taking the piss, but it wasn't. This was how the officers lived. The food was great, too, all week. They eat pretty well because of the nature of the job, so we didn't eat much differently from them. Weight training commenced at 8.30 a.m., after which Clive handed us over to the Marines who kitted us out with fatigues, waterproofs, backpacks, rifles, magazines – the whole shebang. Our emergency rations came in a six-inch square by six-inch deep box: lots of vacuum-packed pasta and chicken, ham, treacle pudding, chocolate, Kendal mint-cake and biscuits. You could eat it cold or boil it up. It was mainly for use on Dartmoor if the helicopters couldn't come in to pick us up for any reason. For the first couple of days nobody touched the rations but as it got closer to going home the food began to disappear.

We were divided into groups. Mine was Yellow Group, comprising Neil Back, Matt Dawson, David Rees, Jason Leonard, Danny Grewcock and Matt Perry. Each group had its own instructor – ours was known to us quite simply as 'Coops', and he was a top man.

The helicopter ride on to Dartmoor was exciting enough for starters, flying in low to follow the lie of the land, up the river valleys, so as to get in and out as fast as possible, just like in wartime. They dumped us in the middle of Dartmoor at a place called Foggin Tor, a large granite quarry. Here we did some abseiling; death slides down a rope attached to the cliff face of the quarry; and then commando 'run downs' where your abseiling harness is worn back to front so you can literally run down the cliff face.

Some of the activities pitted the team against the clock. For example, we had to climb a cliff face, run over a hill and down the other side to erect a military tent, before running back and abseiling down the cliff. The ethos was for the team to work together and stay together. Another exercise involved changing the wheel of a Land Rover and getting it under cover inside 30 minutes because there was supposed to be an air raid. You begin by radioing the stores for the necessary kit. When it arrives, of course, it's the wrong kit, isn't it? So you have to improvise and work out how to make the best of what you've got. Eventually we hoiked up the Land Rover with some poles and some blocks to change the wheel successfully.

We still weren't finished. Next was a four-kilometre yomp across the moor, during which we were supposed to pick up certain things *en route*: first it was telegraph poles and rope; then it was 30-kilo water containers; the poles and rope were to construct a stretcher to carry these cans up a massive hill where you were to be met by the helicopter. The day ended at 11 p.m. It was off to Portsmouth for some food at 11.45 and bed at half-past midnight. The only trouble was we had to be up again at 5 a.m.!

Tuesday saw us depart at 6.15 a.m. for a series of stress tests, where the pressure was more mental than physical, at HMS Raleigh, a shore establishment nearby. We reached the place by boat, one of those eight-seater things where you just straddle a seat and hold on for dear life. With the seas quite rough, the ride was exhilarating, especially as you had a 20lb pack on your back and you were trying to keep your feet dry. No chance! They stop the boat offshore, don't they!

The base looks like a couple of two-storey portakabins but inside it was just like a ship, with hatches and ladders. The first exercise was the fire chamber. The room was full of thick, black smoke – supposedly an oil fire that you had to put out. We are all decked out in fire-protective gear, masks and air tanks, but you can't see a thing, not even your hand in front of your face, because the smoke is so dense. The only way you can do the job is to stick together, touch and signal. I had to lead the group down a ladder like a human chain and then feel my way along the wall until I found another ladder or a hatch and finally reached the bottom where the fire was. The instructor was waiting for us at the bottom and passed out the fire extinguishers. When everybody had one the group was meant to open fire. I was in charge for this test so I had to ask the last man in the line if he'd got his extinguisher before giving the order to fire. He said, 'Yes,' so I shouted 'Fire!' Unfortunately, the guy one from the tail – I think it was David Rees – hadn't got his and the instructor was standing there trying to sort him out. Of course, I let off my extinguisher, which hit the fire, sent a fireball to the ceiling and gave the poor instructor a faceful of fire! Needless to say, that did not go down very well.

The exercise lasted 30 to 40 minutes and was pretty hair-raising. It was all about trusting the guy next to you in the knowledge that if you cock up, he'll die. If you don't do the job right, the guy next to you is going to be in a lot of trouble – which relates to the rugby field, doesn't it? One group, I think, did become separated and I believe Phil de Glanville and Neil McCarthy, for example, found themselves in bother.

Although that was bad enough, it was the next test that really frightened the shit out of me. This was a tunnel maze, full of water, which you had to negotiate blindfolded – the masks we wore were blacked out. The spaces were very confined and, being my size, I had an awful feeling I'd get stuck somewhere. Halfway down one tunnel you meet a beam. You can't go over it. You must go under, which means under water. For how long, you've no idea. It could be a second or it could be 30 seconds. You're wearing breathing apparatus but I still found this petrifying. I was following Jason Leonard, holding his boots. At one stage I lost him for a moment. I'm on my hands and knees, up to my belly in water, scared to death. My eyes are tight shut because if you keep them open you become dizzy and nauseous. Your brain is telling you that you can't see: if your eyes are shut the brain tells you it doesn't matter that you can't see. You can take off the mask at any time and quit but the Marines' philosophy is that no matter how shit-scared you are, you keep going, working as a team. After we'd finished, we looked at the set-up and it was no more intimidating than a kiddies' playground!

The final two stress tests were not quite so harrowing. One involved escaping from a foam-filled tank in chemical warfare kit; your overalls are white when you go in and black when you come out! Lastly, we did this shipwreck simulation where you are trying to shore up the holes in a sinking vessel before finally being forced to evacuate it. You have to keep diving underwater with a mallet and wedges to plug the holes. You work for 40 minutes, absolutely flat out, and when the water gets up to your chest, they shout: 'Abandon ship!'

It was well into the afternoon before we had to carry out an amphibious assault on a fort defended by some of the recruits. It's a bit toy-soldierish but the thought of doing it for real was daunting enough. This took us to eight or nine in the evening, when the sight of the helicopters coming in was absolute bliss. But they'd another trick up their sleeves. They said we were being taken off to do a five-kilometre run. We had to give them a time in which the group would complete it and a helicopter would be waiting for us. If we weren't there in the specified time, the helicopter would leave without us. Of course, we were all completely knackered by that point but, unbeknown to us, we weren't actually going to have to do the run. They were telling us we had to do it in order to gauge our reactions. The Marines call it 'dislocated expectations' – nobody ever knows what they are going to have to do because they might get to a certain point and find the situation has changed. For instance, in the Gulf War the Marines were told they had to run ten kilometres to reach a helicopter – only to find it wasn't there. They had to run a further ten kilometres. They did this nine times before they actually got picked up. They work you to the point of fatigue but you must keep going because in wartime you die if you don't. It's like the last five minutes of a match: you're knackered, you think you've won, the opposition come again – but you've got the capacity to pick yourself up and get back into the game.

Wednesday morning was free – in anticipation of the assault course and 'mud run' at 1.30 p.m. We were to be timed and the aim was to finish it in around 15 minutes. The Marines complete it in 14. We were, in fact, the fastest group. All the while gunfire and grenades were going off. You begin by picking up two heavy water drums and some ammunition boxes which you push in front of you through a 30-foot tunnel. You reach an ambulance containing a body (some overalls filled with rocks), which you have to push – because it isn't working – up and down some hills until you get to the assault course proper. The object then is to transport the equipment over a six-foot wall, across the monkey bars, some bridges and back through a tunnel to a swimming-pool, where you're up to your neck in water. Finally, the stretcher must be carried into the mud run – ankle-deep, foul-smelling, squelchy stuff on the Exe estuary. The secret of this was never to step in someone else's old foot-hole because the mud's already six inches deep in it, and you'd go in another six inches and get stuck. This happened to Daz, who had to be rescued. We took by far the longest route but because we chose virgin mud we didn't sink as much as everyone else.

The afternoon ended with us helping out with some rugby coaching of a group of primary-school kids who were having a tag-rugby tournament. The last evening we shared a barbecue and a few beers with all the instructors. On the Thursday morning they presented each of us with a photo album to remind us of what we'd been through – and that was that. We'd been so busy it felt like we'd been there a fortnight.

An awful lot had been crammed into those three days, and although it was obviously exceptionally physical, it was the mental pressure that took the greater toll. Each activity had a different IC within the group and whatever he said, you did: mine was the fire chamber. The Marines soon assess who are leaders and who are followers; who are humpers and who are thinkers. Each night all the Marine team leaders, like Coops, held a debriefing session with Clive and our management. From what I could gather, the findings were pretty much what the management already knew about us.

The Marines were something else. They were so disciplined they didn't give a toss what the conditions were or what was happening around them. They blot out everything. You'd think they must be fitter than us but in conversation they admitted they probably weren't. It was just a case of when things began to hurt they switched off mentally and kept going. They've had recruits, apparently, who had had stress fractures in their legs yet who were so determined to finish the course that they continued until their legs broke!

Training camps like this one are extremely valuable. You get to see your team-mates in a totally different situation and learn what kind of person they really are. If you only meet them to train before a Five Nations game, play and then disperse, you don't get to know the person all that well. I see the Leicester guys in all sorts of different situations and consequently know how they react, but someone like Jason Leonard, for instance, whom I've played a number of games alongside, I've only ever seen in that particular environment. To see Jason in a roomful of fire or hanging off a cliff is a completely different scenario and allows you to see him in a different light. It's the same for all of us. Are you the sort of person who digs in and gets on with it, or are you the sort who stands back?

That week with the Marines was a break with routine and we were all the better for it.

THIRTEEN

WOODY'S ENGLAND

FIRST and foremost Clive Woodward is a man-manager. Although he obviously has an input into how England play the game he is essentially a man-manager – he's a very successful businessman – who has put together a group of coaches who are among the best in the business: Dave Reddin handles the fitness; Dave Alred is the kicking coach; Phil Larder coaches defence; Brian Ashton coaches the backs and John Mitchell does the forwards. Out on the training pitch the coaches coach and Woody takes a back seat.

In comparison to the Jack Rowell era, Woody is a million miles ahead in the way he treats players and the way new players are integrated into the squad. It's hard to criticise Jack Rowell because he was very successful and I didn't have much to do with him, but the training now compared to when I began my England career under Jack is a different world. The amount of detail we go into now is unbelievable. The game has moved on a helluva lot, and in today's environment I doubt whether Jack Rowell would be as successful as he was a few years back when his record proved he was a very good coach. Money is no object to Woody. If the team want something – laptop computers, new kit, anything – he'll go to the RFU and get it. And if the whole thing goes belly-up he'll take the blame regardless of the consequences, which is a big plus point for him in the eyes of the players.

Woody has his own personal vision of how the game should be played. Some of it is realistic and some of it less so. I like him a lot – he's a genuine bloke and a real team guy – but he is prone to changing his mind very quickly on some matters if he thinks a better way has come up. He's very keen to listen to other people, which occasionally causes him to be influenced too easily. One minute he wants one thing and the next minute something completely different. It can get a bit confusing for the players, who are constantly having to adapt. For example, out in Australia and immediately after we returned, the way we were training was concentrating on what we would do when we'd won the ball. We rarely practised winning the ball in the first place. The fundamentals of the game are the set-pieces, so from a forward's point of view the way we were trying to play the game – not taking on anyone up front – made us feel redundant. From scrum and lineout the ball just got wanged from one side of the pitch to the other and you never did anything with it. With the strong pack we've got, with the ability to take the ball up, we were being nullified. We were constantly offloading the ball and never taking anyone on, which is how we'd played Australia over there in the summer and lost.

Since then things have changed a little. Clive does change tack, sometimes on a whim: somebody says something or he spots something and he'll suddenly change the emphasis. We just about got the balance right in the end between playing this all-singing all-dancing globetrotting game and one involving a few double-shunts from the scrum or some back-row moves. It is great to want to play the game at speed all the time but there are occasions when the forwards have got to do the forwards' jobs and grind it out. Sometimes, that's what wins you the game – battering your opponents into submission. Clive wasn't too keen on seeing that, kicking to the corners and doing scrums, though he gradually became more accommodating.

I always knew that if the game went this way there are players better equipped than me to play that style of rugby. I'm not daft. If someone wants a hooker to do all the set-piece jobs – scrummage, lineout, ruck, maul, tackle – I'm the man. But someone like Phil Greening is a player more suited to the all-singing all-dancing runaround game. However, against the really top sides in the world, by the time you've been scrummaged to death, there's not a lot left in your legs to run around with, so if you're not extremely good at the basics and you're too knackered to do the flashier stuff, your game is nullified completely. I'd rather do the simple things well, which allows the rest of the team to play – which is how it works at Leicester. I can understand Clive's views: if you play a slow, methodical game it is easier to defend against and you're not going to beat the big sides consistently, but there has to be a balance between playing sevens-style rugby and a forward-dominated style.

In my view rugby is a very simple game. Forwards must do the forwards' jobs extremely well. We've built a pack of forwards that's very good, as good as any around, but Woody occasionally asks us to do things that are alien to us. I know we want to play a 'whole' game but we need to do the basics properly and let the expansive stuff come as and when the game opens up after we've worn the opposition down. Woody would rather play, for want of a better term, fancy-dan seat-of-the-pants rugby from the first minute. We shouldn't abandon the strengths of a pack like ours just for the sake of it. For instance, certain players are picked to do certain jobs and then Woody moves the goalposts and asks them to do other things. On balance it's not always a bad thing, but taken from one extreme to the other it can be confusing and ultimately frustrating. Woody is a very bright, intelligent bloke and he thinks everyone thinks on his wavelength. Perhaps he doesn't always remember that all 15 of us possess differing mentalities. Mine is simple: I want to work hard and do my job, which is running into people, hitting rucks and mauls, scrummaging, whereas he sometimes wants me to be a ball-player as well, which is not really part of my game. He picked me to do a particular job but now he wants me to do a slightly different job that is foreign to me. The overall result of this shifting emphasis was that during the Australian Test it got to the stage where the forwards didn't really know what their job was. Running around with the ball in hand and not committing everyone to rucks and mauls is great, but if you don't get the fundamentals of forward play done right, nothing else operates effectively.

Eventually all the talking has to stop and you decide on the way to play. You get to a situation where the coaches say 'we do this' and the players get on with it. That's the best way. Talking is not exactly a waste of time but too much opinion being expressed and absorbed into the strategy can be detrimental. It's only the players who can't play who want to talk tactics!

As the tournament approached, match practice was vital. All our training camps – in Australia, with the Marines or at Twickenham – were beneficial certainly, but we needed games. All of us were playing for our World Cup spots. Normally when you are being considered for England selection you will have had a tough pre-season followed by six or so matches in the Premiership. On this occasion we'd not played for ten weeks. Woody had arranged four matches for us, internationals against the USA and Canada followed by two games against a Premiership Allstars XV. I was not involved in the USA match – not even on the bench – which was won 106–8. The USA have never been a particularly strong side, so it was a good game for us to start with. Canada, on the other hand, are a good side but because we beat them quite comfortably by 36–11 (I came off the bench later on) people said we should have met tougher opposition. This is a little harsh because Canada have had some good results against quality sides. Clive had wanted us to play against two England A selections after that but this proved impossible to arrange and the idea of an Allstars selection, to include all the foreign boys playing over here, was substituted instead. Unfortunately the Premiership clubs weren't too keen and a lot of quality players – Bunce, Carling and Pienaar, for example – dropped out. We beat both sides very easily and immediately faced criticism for not having taken on stronger opposition. But not many people were complaining about the opposition before those games, and Zinzan Brooke actually said in the papers that he thought his particular Allstars side was good enough to take us. I can understand people saying they weren't sufficiently testing opposition but which sides do you play? I would doubt if any of the top sides would wish to play friendlies against each other immediately prior to the World Cup. New Zealand wouldn't want to come and play us three weeks before they met us in the tournament, would they? Or Wales or France for that matter. I know the southern-hemisphere countries played each other but that was because of the Tri-Nations competition and they had no choice. If New Zealand, South Africa and Australia could have hand-picked their warm-up games I don't think they'd have chosen each other.

It was difficult to focus against the Premiership sides. You know half the lads but you don't know how they're going to play. There are no videos of previous encounters to assess strengths and weaknesses. It's all a bit up in the air. We decided on a particular style of play, therefore, and hoped it would work. It did, inasmuch as we won comfortably, but mistakes were inevitably made. My first throw in the Twickenham match, for instance, went straight to Tony Diprose instead of to my intended target and gifted the Allstars an immediate try. One or two other throws had gone astray in those matches which pointed the finger at me. People in the stands always assume it's the thrower's fault but in some of these instances the lifting wasn't spot on, for instance after Danny Grewcock came on for Tim Rodber. Needless to say, Stuart Barnes seemed to relish the opportunity to have a go at me. On Sky he said Phil Greening should definitely start the World Cup as number-one hooker and in *The Daily Telegraph* he wrote that the pace of the new England style was too fast for me and that if Clive chose me ahead of Greening it would be his first mistake of the World Cup. It looked like he was trying his hardest to sow enough seeds of doubt to get me dropped.

For the final three weeks of our preparation before our first World Cup game, against Italy on 2 October, we were based at the Petersham Hotel in Richmond, training at Twickenham or Imber Court. Home advantage in all three of our Group fixtures was a crucial advantage so it would be stupid not to capitalise upon it by training at Twickenham and getting used to the surroundings.

Training was just as intense as usual but a lot shorter in duration. We'd worked so hard previously that it was no longer necessary to flog ourselves, and the emphasis was much more on technical aspects at scrum, lineout, ruck and maul. In particular we worked on clearing bodies off the ball at the tackle as it was felt we'd been allowing the opposition to slow the ball up; we concentrated on knocking opponents past the ball in order to give the scrum-half quick ball. In between, we'd have some team-runs to highlight the strengths and weaknesses of our Group opponents – Italy, New Zealand and Tonga. There wasn't much time for any laughing or joking now. It's difficult to have a light atmosphere in a tense situation, isn't it? We'd enjoy a game of football to warm up, perhaps a game of head tennis, and the SAQ (speed, agility, quickness) sessions could be more lighthearted, but everything else was deadly serious. You get your enjoyment in these circumstances by doing everything well, not by fooling about and becoming sloppy.

Rugby became even more all-consuming, difficult though that was. Some of the London lads with families would be allowed home for 24 hours but for most of us the Petersham became home – or a prison, depending on your point of view. Occasionally we'd get out into Richmond, which is full of antique shops so I was kept happy! On Wednesdays we'd go out for a meal, a Chinese or a Mexican. Some of us – Nick Beal, Joe Worsley, Martyn Wood, Daz Garforth – celebrated Leon Lloyd's 22nd birthday with a Chinese; Daz, Jase Leonard, Lawrence Dallaglio, Jerry Guscott and I went to the cinema one night to see the new shark movie, *Deep Blue Sea* – though the highlight of that was being able to eat some chocolate without being spotted! And there were various PR jobs to do, such as a couple of World Cup send-off dinners, one at Grosvenor House on Park Lane and another at the Café Royal, attended by corporations that had supported us. The RFU had apparently received £20,000 for the entire squad to attend, each one of us allocated to a different table. I think I was with Barclays Bank for one and Schroders, the financial company, for the other.

We were also on the receiving end. Clive is big on listening to other people talking about their approach to things, such as the Marines. He'd been friendly with Steve Redgrave for a while and got him to talk to us for an hour or so before he flew out to Australia for a training camp. Now, rowing is not a favourite sport of mine but this man is a legend and was worth listening to. Olympic titles, World titles – the lot. We all gave him the utmost respect. He pointed out some parallels between his sport and ours. His peak races may be wide apart but every time he rows people are trying to knock him off his perch, which is exactly what happens when international rugby players return to club rugby. Consequently, he must maintain a huge pride in his own perfor-mance. He also spoke about what keeps him motivated after all those years at the top. He referred to some race, a World Cham-pionship I think, where he'd rowed the first half as hard as he could and, coming to the third quarter, he was absolutely shot to bits. He looked across to see another boat level. He thought to himself, if I'm knackered, they must be just as knackered, so I'll give it ten strokes all out – and he pulled ahead.

It's the same on the rugby field if it's 18-all with ten minutes to play, isn't it? Mentally, you have to keep digging in, knowing the opposition are feeling as bad as you. He also told us how he was criticised in his early career because he wouldn't row with anyone who didn't devote the same dedication to the sport as he does. His view is that he doesn't want to flog his guts out beside someone who only puts in half the effort he does. It's like ten guys training really hard in a rugby team and five not bothering. They let the side down. Everyone must pull together. We got the message.

Despite the backbiting from pressmen like Stuart Barnes, I was selected for the opening World Cup game against Italy. We'd been given a few days off after the second Allstars game and the side was announced at a team meeting as soon as we reported back to the Petersham. The team was pretty much as expected apart from Phil de Glanville in the centre instead of Jerry Guscott, who was carrying a slight injury and would be on the bench. Phil Vickery got the tight-head spot ahead of Daz, and Danny Grewcock was preferred to Tim Rodber in the second row. We'd watched Argentina push Wales very close in the tournament's opening game and were not sure what to expect, as we were playing similar opposition. We had narrowly beaten Italy 22–15 in Huddersfield the previous autumn when they were a good side. They'd struggled for form since but it preyed on our minds that we could start the World Cup at Twickenham before a full house and only scrape home by a few points. Italy are a difficult side to play against in that they try to kill the ball a lot to slow the game down. They're ill-disciplined and don't mind conceding penalties. That's why we'd worked so hard on clearing rucks and presenting the ball efficiently. You have to be very disciplined yourself against an untidy side like Italy because you must control the ball in possession or they will live off the scraps, the turnovers, the crooked lineouts and the knock-ons. You must keep the pressure on them by eliminating errors and then they will start to panic, get annoyed with each other and invariably concede penalties.

There was definitely more emotion in the dressing-room before the match than there would be for an ordinary game against Italy.

We'd been waiting a long time for this moment. Clive's parting words were no different from usual: 'We've prepared well. We're fit, we're strong. We've got the talent on the pitch. Believe in what we're trying to do and just play!' Johnno was just Johnno: 'Front up! Do your job!' That's his final line. Nothing scientific. Let's get out there and do it!

The game couldn't have gone better for us. Italy started hard and fast but we soon found our stride; Jonny Wilkinson kicked an early penalty and after only ten minutes Matt Dawson snaffled a try. After that it was plain sailing. We could have beaten them by outmuscling them, kicking and winning by ten or fifteen points. But, the way we're playing nowadays, Italy ended up chasing shadows. We killed them off straight away and against inferior opposition we now rack up lots of points. We thrashed them 67–7, scoring eight tries, with Jonny Wilkinson converting six as well as kicking five penalties. And we didn't miss one lineout!

I came off after 51 minutes with a cut finger – which is a story in itself. Phil Greening was always going to replace me at some stage but with only Martin Corry on the bench to cover both the second and back rows, Clive wanted to take me off for 'blood' just in case it was necessary to bring me back on. They were going to cut me at half-time so I could come off. However, the previous Saturday, before we'd reported back, I'd been at home doing some jobs around the house. We were about to have a new bathroom fitted and I decided I might as well remove the old tiles. Being me, I couldn't be bothered with gloves and goggles, any of that safety crap. I'm banging away and promptly cut my finger on a broken tile. That afternoon I went down to Welford Road to watch the club play Sale and showed the cut to our doc, Dave Finlay. He puts four stitches in, doesn't he! So in the Italy game there was no need to pretend. The doc just looked at my finger and opened up the stitches.

The following Saturday was the big one, New Zealand. Ever since the draw had been made, this was the game everyone had been waiting for and building up to. The winner would gain an automatic quarter-final slot. The loser would have to qualify via a play-off and then face the gruelling prospect of having to beat probably South Africa and Australia in order to get another crack at the winners in the final.

The build-up to the match followed the normal approach, although it was difficult to pinpoint any weaknesses in their game. After a shaky start against Tonga the Blacks eventually ran out winners 45–9, with Mr Lomu grabbing a couple of tries. To beat them we'd have to get the basics right. John Mitchell was an All Black and was therefore able to impart some insights into their mentality, what they like and what they don't like. You must take the game to them. If you are in awe of the Blacks and sit back, they'll destroy you. You have to be in their faces, competing and being as physical and as nasty and as cocksure as they are. When you take them on they are like any other side in the world. They have to tackle, they'll get offside, they'll give away penalties, holes will appear in their defence. Our forwards would take the ball up, drive the lineouts, keep the pace of the game high, never allow them to rest or give them time to compose themselves and maintain their organisation. Everyone became grumpier and snappier in training whenever a mistake was made because we all knew how critical any errors and turnovers could become in what was bound to be a tight contest. The only change in the side was Jerry Guscott for Will Greenwood, who was carrying a slight strain.

The atmosphere on match day was the best I've ever experienced with England. I received loads of goodwill messages, including a card from Graham Dawe – though nothing from Mooro! The route from Richmond to Twickenham was absolutely chock-a-block with people all waving flags and banners. On Richmond Bridge there was this tramp, or homeless person, sitting by the side of the road, all filthy and scruffy, and even he stood up and clapped as we passed by. You could feel the tension in the dressing-room. Nothing special was being said or done to generate it, but just as you can sense an atmosphere when you enter a room where someone's in a bad mood, you could feel it there all the time. An air of anxiety, concentration, nervousness: confident but anxious. Many of us had played against the Blacks before – this was my fifth game against them – so we were not apprehensive. We just wanted to get out there and do the job we'd been preparing for. 'Don't sit back and let them play,' Woody kept telling us. 'These guys are not as good as they're made out to be.'

After my headline-grabbing performance during the Haka prior to the Old Trafford Test of 1997, a lot of media attention had been focused on what would happen this time round. The rumours were that the Blacks were going to perform a new, souped-up version and, to avoid any possible ruckus, both teams were told by the authorities to stay on their respective ten-metre lines. We came out in our tracksuits, the idea being that after facing the Haka we'd walk off the pitch to take our tops off, thus wasting a bit of time so they couldn't feed off the adrenaline they'd just raised. Well, me and a few others – Phil Vickery, for one – took ours off straight away. Some people even thought I did this so I'd stand out in the photographs, but anyone who knows me knows I never wear a tracksuit top even in training. I hate wearing layers.

We'd warmed up and I was roasting hot. I couldn't wait to take it off.

We lined up on the halfway line and they began to come towards us. My old mucker Norm Hewitt was no longer in the squad, so the skipper, Taine Randell, led the Haka. The ref, Peter Marshall of Australia, told us to move back. We said, 'Bollocks. We're staying here. Get them back!' He looked at them and they weren't going to budge, so he told us again. 'Make them f***ing move!' we said. Everyone makes allowances for the Blacks, and the ref hadn't the balls to take them on. We could have just walked away and left them to it, in which case we'd have been accused of showing no respect. One side did that to them down in Wales one year and Buck Shelford followed them right down to their posts where they were in their own huddle before commencing the Haka. And I bet if we'd done something similar at Twickenham they'd have followed us – and got away with it in spite of all the pre-match instructions. Everyone is frightened of the All Blacks, especially referees. The whole thing is a load of rubbish, really. Anyway, Johnno couldn't give a toss, so he gave a couple of metres and then we edged back forward again.

I've never played in a game that's been so quick and so physical, not against South Africa, Australia or the previous New Zealand Tests. The intensity of the hits was enormous. I took the ball up on one occasion and got pulverised. And our hits were just as big – there were times when they were complaining to the referee. We actually dominated them. The game stats showed we had 65 per cent of the possession and 63 per cent territorial advantage; we won 73 rucks to their 21 and won the ball 80 times in open play to their 24. And yet we lost 16–30. Why? How? Most people will answer with two words: Jonah Lomu.

We fell behind early after Jonny Wilkinson missed a couple of penalties and Jeff Wilson had scored in the corner but ten minutes into the second half we had clawed our way back to 16-all and the tide was definitely turning in our favour. With 20 minutes to go we had them rocking. We had them on the ropes but didn't finish them off. Then Lomu scores – and it was our error that set things up for him. It was a fantastic try from fully 55 metres out, reminiscent of the one he scored against England in the 1995 World Cup semi-final. It was testimony to his tremendous ability but we gave him the extra space he'd been denied up to that point in the match. We turned the ball over going forward, which meant our backs' alignment was deep whereas theirs was flat. Suddenly Mehrtens throws out a lovely long pass to Lomu with our backs 30 metres away. Once he's got up his head of steam, which doesn't take long, he takes some stopping. He's immensely big and immensely quick: he's 18 stone and quicker than Jerry Guscott or Austin Healey. Fourteen-stoners waiting for an 18-stone man running at full pelt is no contest. He just brushed aside Jerry and Austin – who's one of our best defenders – as if they weren't there. Lomu is a freak of nature, isn't he? He's been born naturally big and naturally quick, characteristics of many South Sea Islanders. It's nothing to do with weight-training or diet. It's a natural set of gifts that we don't possess and New Zealand are lucky to have him in their team.

Lomu can be tackled one on one: Matt Perry proved that if you go low and hold on he'll have to come down – and Pezza is only 14 stone wringing wet. It's tempting to make special provision for Lomu but this can potentially be dangerous. If you give Jonah too much attention his fellow backs profit. If he was a member of, with all due respect, an Irish or Scottish team, for instance, you could possibly put two or three men on him to knock him over knowing damn well that when they recycle the ball they haven't the talent to exploit the extra space. You can't do that with New Zealand because they've got Wilson, Cullen or Umaga waiting for the ball and they're all awesome players in their own right. You never know – had we kept that ball in contact and kicked down-field to force a scrum or lineout near their line, we might have created a turnover for ourselves that resulted in a score. It's a fine line between success and failure, isn't it? Perhaps if you take Lomu out of their team – and he was the gamebreaker in a close match – the eventual result may have been different. I know the Blacks scored another converted try before the final whistle but Lomu's try was the killer blow because it came when we appeared to be in the driving seat. We could have won the game. I'm not saying we *should* have won the game but the chances were there to do so.

I expected to play for probably 50 or 60 minutes but was on for 71. We needed to be strong at scrum and lineout and be physical at ruck and maul, which is what I contribute to the team. A third try with ten minutes to go meant we trailed by 14 points and fresh legs were beneficial. Had we been ahead I'm sure I'd have stayed on. Although I'd rather play the full 80, I don't particularly resent doing the graft, the hard yards, at the start of games before coming off. You do feel aggrieved coming off at times if things have been going well but the way we are playing – it's so fast and so physical up front – and with quality players, 'change players' as Woody likes to call them, on the bench, I take it as a compliment to my ability, as a scrummager for instance, that I'm asked to take the brunt of what the opposition has to offer. Phil Greening is talented, like Keith Wood, around the pitch and he's young and fresh, not having played a lot of rugby over the last year or two because of injury.

The way the game is played today, front-row forwards can't always expect to last a game. We are told to play eyeballs-out for as long as we can and when we're shot we come off. It's a 22-man game these days, and Clive is keen to utilise the strengths of all of us.

Stuart Barnes seized the opportunity to criticise me once again, saying I lost control mentally when it mattered; that I packed 'more of a waddle than a wallop'; and that Greening made a much greater impact in the ten minutes he was on than I had all game. When I've been scrummaging my balls off for 70 minutes and making hits, I think a fresh Phil Greening is going to be a lot more active than 15 All Blacks who've been getting battered for as long as I had. It's no reflection on Phil to say that, because that's what he's there to do, but one-eyed people like Barnes should be ignored. Our lineout, especially my throwing, was described as 'awful': New Zealand's was 'polished'. And yet we won 13 of our 16 throws; they won 10 out of 14. The stats for the whole tournament showed my throwing at over 90 per cent – the second best in the competition. So it makes no sense to me. Yes, I did get done for two not-straights, one of which got them into the game with a scrum 40 metres from our line when really it should have been our possession. It was a massive game and I was at fault, so obviously it was very frustrating. But the lineouts throughout the tournament had already been very competitive – Samoa and Fiji robbing balls off Wales and France, for example – and the referees had been instructed to tighten up. It was only three days before the tournament started that they changed the lifting law from legs to shorts. All in all, the critics were waiting to stick the knife into me, so I shouldn't have been surprised when they did.

There was also some criticism of our back play. Just think what New Zealand would have done with all that possession, was the main thrust of the argument. Well, our back line was the best available so I'm not going to blame them. Certainly, a lot of our most incisive running came from our forwards but you can't be one-dimensional. If you don't use your backs, you're easy to play against; one-up, bash-up rugby won't beat the southern-hemisphere sides more than once out of ten. Maybe our backs aren't as good as theirs. They have more bulk than us and are therefore able to play a more direct game. I'm sure we are as skilful as them individually, but they possess size as well as skill. Perhaps they are superior collectively. Never mind. We must still aim to play 15-man rugby because that is what wins the big matches.

FOURTEEN

THE END OF THE ROAD

WE had the Sunday free – wives and girlfriends stayed over – and Woody told us not to bring the New Zealand game with us when we reported on Monday. We were still a good side, despite what any of the press said, in the world's top two or three. We'd been very close to turning the All Blacks over. Now we had to beat Tonga to reach the play-off for a quarter-final place. The Tongans were known to be very physical and some of the South Africans – our likely quarter-final opponents – were quoted as saying they thought the Tongans would cause some casualties. This sort of talk cheesed us off a bit, I can tell you.

I badly wanted to play but I knew there were bound to be changes because we were now likely to be playing three games in nine days. Woody selected Phil Greening to start and also replaced Jonny Wilkinson, Jase Leonard, Backy and Danny Grewcock. At the press conference he said this was a full-strength side, so the next day the papers were full of 'Wilkinson axed' and 'Cockerill dropped'. That day, after training at Imber Court, he sat us all down and said he'd messed up at the press conference and should have said some guys were being rested and that the team which started against New Zealand was his first-choice XV. There's not one player in our squad who couldn't get into the Tongan side, so we could have changed the whole 15 if we'd wanted to. We all knew that, although none of us would say so before the game. The result speaks for itself: we won 101–10. I came on after 60 minutes for Lawrence Dallaglio, with Greening going into the back row. It was that straightforward.

The only real talking point of the game was the incident which led to the Tongan prop Taufo'ou being sent off. Matt Perry went up for a high ball and Tapueluelu, the flanker, tackled him in mid-air, turning Pezza over so that he landed on his head. Even so, Pezza, who's got a big heart on him, still kept hold of the ball despite being half dead on the floor! Phil Vickery then came in to push the Tongan away but this guy Taufo'ou charges in and whacks Richard Hill with a forearm smash to the back of the head! Hilly was only a bystander! I've never seen him even throw a punch in all the games I've played with or against him. On the bench we all thought the original tackler has gotta go. He actually stood over Pezza for a while, in a menacing sort of way, before Phil arrived on the scene. I'm sure he would have got his marching orders from the referee, Wayne Erickson, had the second guy not got involved, instead of just a yellow card. Phil Vickery also got yellow-carded and although there were demands for him to be cited he escaped further punishment.

The whole citing procedure at the World Cup was a shambles. Grau and Charvis were cited after the first game, Argentina v Wales, for a few jabs – which is nothing – and they got three weeks' suspension. Kicking or mindless stamping, like Venter got done for against Uruguay, is one thing, but this was nothing outrageous. In a physical game like rugby, tempers do get frayed and the odd punch will be thrown. It's boys being boys, spur-of-the-moment stuff. If it's cowardly blindsiding or a cheap shot then that needs tougher punishment, but a bust-up at a scrum or a lineout is part and parcel of the game. It gets rid of the tension in any case. Banning guys for a few punches is stupid.

Phil Greening scored two tries against Tonga, unfortunately for me, and Woody kept him in the side for the play-off with Fiji – although the selection was again noticeably not the strongest XV. It's very difficult being on the bench at this level. You're out of it, really. You're not quite as mentally into training all week. You try to stay positive to help the boys out. For example, we'll discuss what Fiji might do from an attacking lineout, go away and practise it for 20 minutes and then go through it against the team so they can prepare for the real thing in the match. You warm up as normal on match day but leave the team to itself for the final three or four minutes before tagging on to the end of the line when they come out. You're up for the game but not in the same intense way as usual. I didn't want Greening to be 'man of the match' but I shook his hand and said, 'Have a good 'un – do the basics well.' I wanted him to play well enough for us to go through. There was a quarter-final place to play for, when I might be back in the starting line-up. And there were the financial considerations of getting through to remember!

Woody told me I'd get on after 50 minutes or so. Once that stage passes and you're not on, that's usually it. I eventually came on after 70, with the game obviously done and dusted. But the big thing about it was that it enabled me, Daz and Graham to pack down together in a full international for the first time. Daz played from the start and Graham had come on early for Jase Leonard. It was a great achievement for the three of us, albeit dampened slightly because Graham and I didn't start. We were mightily chuffed, though. The moment was sweet. We never thought it would happen even in this age of multi replacements. Certainly Woody is no sentimentalist who would put us together just for the sake of it. It would have been even nicer in a bigger Test but it was quite possibly the last chance we'll have. For a variety of different reasons, I think it is safe to say that our days at international level may be numbered. We nearly ended up swapping our shirts with the Fijians before finally realising the implications. We might want a testimonial one day and these three shirts, signed and framed, might fetch a few bob at auction!

With the game safely won 45–24 we travelled to Paris by Eurostar on the Thursday, arriving at one of the Sofitel hotels after what had been a seven-hour journey all told. The food was poor compared to the Petersham, French or not! Training was pretty low-key as most people had played on the Wednesday. The team for Sunday's showdown with South Africa was announced on the Friday and I was not included. I thought I was in with a decent shout of reclaiming my spot, not because Greening had played badly – he hadn't – but because South Africa had a huge pack and it would be the sort of game that suited my capabilities. Du Randt, Drotske and Visagie made up some front row and the scrum was going to be a vital contest. If they dominated the scrum, as they can, the whole Springbok game would gather momentum. Meet the scrum engagement poorly and the hooker tends to find his head between Drotske's and Visagie's as the tight-head bores inwards. Some vice that is!

I was a bit pissed off at not being picked but assumed Woody wanted to play a faster, wider game. When we failed to play that kind of game I was even more pissed off. Why play a forward-oriented game when you've picked runaround players? Perhaps Woody failed to appreciate how the game would unfold. We began well enough, Paul Grayson potting a few penalties, but contrary to the game plan – don't let them back into the game immediately after a score – we let de Beer kick some of his own. We kept kicking it right down Percy Montgomery's throat at full-back and he stuck it 70 metres behind us all the time. We were supposed to be running at them, using Dallaglio and Hill as in the New Zealand game, or, if they were up flat, sticking it in the corners. Even though we won 56 per cent of the possession, we never did this. We played a lot of sideways stuff and failed to launch the big guys at them to score a forwards' try. We never looked like scoring a try and were very lame. It was so wishy-washy, neither a forwards' game nor a backs' game.

It all made for painful viewing in the dugout. I'd been told by Woody I'd come on after 50 or 60 minutes. Just after half-time we were only one point behind at 15–16 and Daz and I were dying to get on, get a buzz going. But Woody stuck to his starters. Then came de Beer's five drop goals and we were on the way out of the tournament, finally losing 21–44. We ran out of steam in the last 20 minutes. Daz, Tim Rodber and I could easily have gone on and improved matters. But Woody makes the decisions and he lives or dies by them.

At the whistle Daz and I walked over to Phil Greening and told him he'd done his best and should have no regrets. The dressing-room was like a morgue, naturally. John Mitchell was close to tears; Johnno was pretty emotional. All Woody said was, 'Some things are meant to be and today was not our day.' There was a crate of Heineken for us but no one felt like a drink. Graham and

I began opening a few bottles, persuaded Jase Leonard to have one, and I went across to Woody, who was talking with Brian Ashton by now, and offered him one. He took it. I felt I should have been more disappointed than I was. I *was* disappointed but not gutted like the lads who'd played. I was more frustrated. When you're playing, it's life and death, isn't it?

Back at the Sofitel all the players, coaches and all the wives had a meeting in the team-room during which Woody thanked each player when he presented him with his World Cup cap. Every squad member got one, even the likes of Leon Lloyd, Neil McCarthy, Martyn Wood and Victor Ubogu who never got on the field throughout the tournament. After that we got packed ready to leave first thing next morning and proceeded to get truly pissed. Some of us who were without our partners – me, Daz, Wig and John Mitchell – eventually made our way into town. All I can recall was leaving Garath Archer in some club at 3.30 in the morning. We never saw him again! He didn't return with the party to England. We got back to Twickenham to pick up our kit and our cars and that was it. No more words. No fancy goodbyes. The end of the road which was meant to see us lift the World Cup.

Woody's position as coach immediately came up for discussion. He'd always said that he should be judged by what happened in the World Cup, which obviously left him open to attack. We'd beaten three lesser sides only to lose both the big games. My main criticism of Woody concerns some of his man-management. I prefer a face-to-face approach. Receiving criticism and team selection by e-mail was something I really resented. Tim Rodber and Jason Leonard were also on the receiving end of this kind of grief. Some of the criticism was quite cutting and nasty, and yet the player can't put his side of the story into the argument. I think it's all a bit gutless, really. I don't say Woody is gutless because he sincerely believes that's the way to do it, but it won't do for me. Two adults ought to be able to discuss things face to face instead of resorting to a one-way conversation – which really does wind me up. Nor did anyone explain to me why I wasn't picked to play against Tonga, Fiji or South Africa. It can't do any harm to be told, can it?

Nevertheless, I think Woody's done a good job on the whole and I definitely think he should stay on as coach or 'Performance Director', as some are suggesting. We all thought two years would be long enough to create the culture necessary to win the World Cup, but it wasn't. The game of rugby has developed too fast. We have come a long way in Woody's two years but we're still at the start of a long road, trying to catch up with the southern-hemisphere style of play. We could have played the traditional English forwards-dominated game in the World Cup – and perhaps we should have done. Against the big teams I do believe you must play a percentage game, a forwards' game linked to a sound kicking game. Forwards must make the hard yards early on to weaken the opposition and open up the gaps for the backs later on in the game. To beat the big boys on a consistent basis I'm sure you do have to incorporate a wider game. But, at present, we've not got the size in our back line to do so successfully and it might have been wiser to have reverted to type in order to win a World Cup quarter-final against South Africa. And, who knows, if New Zealand had approached our match as they did their semi-final with France, we could have progressed further than we did. Our game with the Blacks had been billed as a crunch match for so long that both sides played as if it were the final itself, whereas the Blacks just turned up expecting to beat what had been a poor

French side. You don't expect to see an All Black team leading 24–10 fall apart, do you? But the French were playing for their lives and deserved to make the final.

If we keep playing the way we have been doing, and continue to develop and nurture the younger players coming through who have benefited from this new mindset since the age of 15 or 16, there's no telling what England can achieve in the future. England's main problem, I feel, is that our players are contracted to the clubs rather than the union – as they are in the southern hemisphere. England has a fantastic club game, second to none, but this means the RFU has no power over players and their development because the clubs own our contracts. The player's first loyalty is to the club that pays him – which also ensures he plays more often than is good for him. The outcome is that the national side suffers in much the same way as the England football team suffers at the hands of the clubs. It would be great, for instance, if England could join the Tri-Nations and play South Africa, Australia and New Zealand home and away every year. With our domestic club programme, I can't see that happening. But it's that sort of regular, intense competition that England require if we are to win a World Cup.

Now the World Cup is over, I can't see much international life left in me. I've played rugby virtually non-stop for three years and some day it's going to catch up with me. It's a dilemma whether to carry on and risk underperforming because I'm tired, or take a voluntary break and forfeit an international place. It's a tricky decision when you're not an automatic member of the squad in the first place. Either way it could well be the end of the international road for yours truly, in which case, the odyssey is over.